Traverse City Postcard History

by Lawrence Wakefield

Acknowledgments

The great majority of the postcards that appear in this book are from the "Postcards from the Attic & the Cellar" collection of Kathi Waggoner Gorski. We want to express our deep gratitude to Mrs. Gorski for allowing us to use them.

Our sincere thanks also to these other postcard contributors: George Happy, Lois Orth, the Con Foster Museum and the Grand Traverse Pioneer & Historical Society.

Revised Edition
Published by Horizon Books, Inc.
Traverse City, Michigan
1999

Copyright© 1991 by Lawrence Wakefield. All rights reserved.
Reproduction in whole or part without written permission is prohibited.

Library of Congress Catalog Card Number: 91-076841
ISBN 0-9618903-3 9

Printed in the USA by Book Crafters, Inc., Chelsea, Michigan

On the cover: Front Street, looking east from Union, early 1900s.

CONTENTS

INTRODUCTION
A Brief History of Traverse City, Michigan 4

1860-1885
Lumbering days 7

1886-1910
Industrial growth; beginning of tourism and fruit farming 18

1911-1930
Decline of industry; further development of tourism and fruit farming 78

1931-1950
Growth of tourism and fruit farming; zero population growth 106

1951-Present
Rapid growth of population, service industries and fruit farming 144

INTRODUCTION
A Brief History of Traverse City

Most northern Michigan towns grew up around a sawmill—pine timber gave them birth. Traverse City was no exception. It got started in 1847, when Capt. Harry Boardman, a prosperous farmer near Naperville, Ill., bought 200 acres of virgin pine timber at the foot of Grand Traverse Bay, and furnished his son Horace with the means to build a sawmill there. Horace and two of three hired hands sailed north from Chicago in his father's sloop, *Lady of the Lake,* and arrived on the site in early June.

With the help of local Indians they finished the sawmill in October of that same year. It stood on the small creek (successively known as Mill Creek, Asylum Creek, and Kids Creek) that empties into the Boardman River at its western loop at Wadsworth Street. The only other settlement in the vast wilderness for miles around was an Indian mission near the tip of the peninsula that separates the two arms of Grand Traverse Bay. It had been established by a Presbyterian missionary, Rev. Peter Dougherty, in 1839.

The little Boardman mill continued to operate through the winter of 1850-'51, but results were disappointing. With its single muley saw, the mill was slow and inefficient, and when the price of lumber plummeted in 1850, Capt. Boardman (the military title was honorary) decided to sell. He found a buyer in the newly organized Chicago lumber firm of Hannah, Lay & Company and its three youthful partners, Perry Hannah, Albert Tracy Lay and James Morgan. Eager to develop their own standing timber resources, Hannah and William Morgan (brother of James) accompanied Capt. Boardman to Grand Traverse Bay aboard the schooner *Venus* in the spring of 1851 and closed the deal. For $4,500 they acquired the sawmill and several small buildings, plus the 200 acres upon which Traverse City now stands.

(It is said that Capt. Boardman was astonished upon arrival to find the mill shut down and all hands playing cards. Horace's explanation that he'd given the men a day off because of a threat of rain convinced the Captain that his decision to sell the property was wise.)

The company lost no time in building a much larger steam mill on the Bay just west of the river's mouth. Over the next thirty-five years it would harvest more than 400 million feet of pine lumber in the Boardman River valley. The lumber was shipped to Chicago in the company's own bottoms—some of it was used to rebuild Chicago after the Great Fire of 1871—and great wealth flowed into the pockets of all four partners. (William Morgan had been added to the partnership in 1852.)

For the first few years, Hannah and Lay alternated every six months as company head in Chicago and Traverse City, but after 1855 Hannah took sole charge of the company in Traverse City and Tracy Lay remained in the windy city.

The village was laid out by Tracy Lay in 1852, and was granted a post office in 1853. During the winter the mail was carried weekly from Manistee in a backpack by an Indian called Old Joe. The first school was established in 1853 with 15-year-old Helen Goodale, daughter of Traverse City's first physician David C. Goodale, as teacher. It was housed in a little log shanty, formerly a stable, on the south side of Front Street, just east of Boardman Avenue.

For the first 15 years the tiny village was completely isolated from the outside world except by boat and Indian trail—and not even by boat in winter. Perry Hannah, elected to the Michigan legislature in 1854, had to make the trip to Lansing that winter on snowshoes, accompanied by an Indian guide. It took them six days.

The first road south, the Northport-Newaygo State Road, was opened in 1864, closely following the old Indian trail. That helped some, but Traverse City's first big "breakout" was the coming of the first railroad, Grand Rapids & Indiana, on November 15, 1872. Whistles blew and churchbells rang and people danced in the street. "Out of the Woods at Last" trumpeted the *Grand Traverse Herald* in banner headlines.

Henry D. Campbell, who had established the first stagecoach lines in the 1860s, built Traverse City's first big hotel, The Park Place, in 1873. The city became a railroad center with the coming of the Chicago and West Michigan (1890), the Manistee & Northeastern (1892), and the Traverse City Leelanau & Manistique (1903). It was incorporated as a village in 1881, and as a city in 1895. Perry Hannah was president of both. (Even during his lifetime Perry Hannah was called the "father of Traverse City.") City water, electricity, and gas lines were established by H. D. Campbell in the late 1880s and '90s. Population reached almost 10,000 in 1900—a ten-year gain of 116%.

But dark clouds had already begun to gather on the horizon. Pine timber was depleted by 1895, and by 1915 so were the hardwoods. Also gone were Traverse City's mainstay industries based on wood and wood products, Its largest employer, Oval Wood Dish Company, for example, pulled up stakes in 1915 and moved to Tupper Lake, NY,, taking with it some 100 worker families and plunging the area into an economic decline that lasted until World War II—when the town seemed empty with all its young men gone, some of whom died in battle and were gone forever.

Traverse City actually lost population in the 1920s and stagnated in the 1930s. It was partly sustained during this period by the Northern Michigan Asylum (later called Traverse City State Hospital), which opened in 1881 under its legendary first superintendent Dr. James Decker Munson. Over the next 70 years it employed an average of 1,000 people, while caring for an estimated 50,000 patients.

But the seeds of resurgence had been sown as early as the 1890s, when the first commercial fruit farms were established and summer people began to spend their vacations at resorts on Grand Bay and the inland lakes. Tourism and fruit farming led the way to Traverse City's phenomenal growth and development during the past 40 years, making it the "World's Cherry Capitol". with its annual National Cherry Festival, and one of the nation's prime tourist attractions.

During that time Traverse City has also become northern Michigan's center for medical care, communications, banking, insurance, government and legal services, shopping and travel, which, along with its great natural beauty, have made it one of the most desirable places in the country to live.

Now, faced with an accelerated pace of growth and development, it has become the primary task of its people to keep it that way.

1860-1885

Load of Logs, Traverse City.   NO. 3784

Load of Hardwood Logs hauled at Honor, near Traverse City, Mich.

Log rollway on the Boardman River.

1847 ~ Traverse City, Mich. - Centennial - June 29 to July 5 ~ 1947

Union Street bridge 1903.

Front Street in 1871.

yright 1905 by the Rotograph Co.

Schooner loading lumber at Traverse City dock.

Grand Traverse Lighthouse was built in 1864.

Early water-powered sawmill on the Boardman River.

Perry Hannah's house on Bay Street.

The Hannah, Lay gristmill, built in 1869, burned down in 1926.

OLD GRIST MILL, TRAVERSE CITY, MICH.

Park Place Hotel was built in 1873 by Henry Campbell.

The first Greilick sawmill, built on the Bay at Division Street in 1871.

Northern Michigan State Hospital was first opened in 1885.

NORTHERN MICHIGAN STATE HOSPITAL, MAIN BUILDING, TRAVERSE CITY, MICH.—5

WILLOW LAKE HOSPITAL GROUNDS, TRAVERSE CITY, MICH.

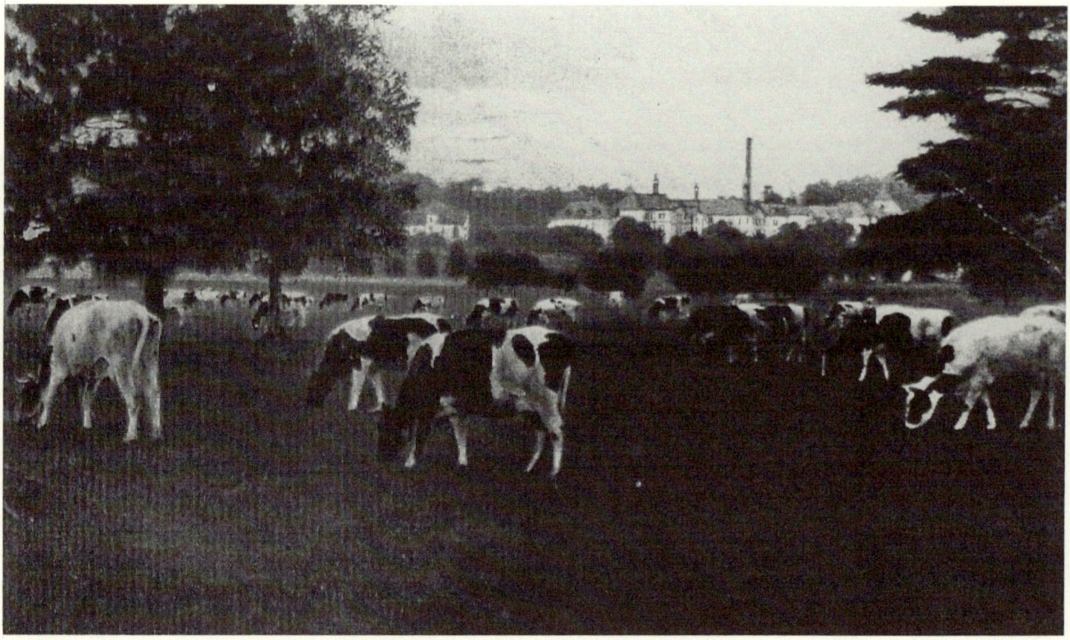

The State Hospital's dairy herd.

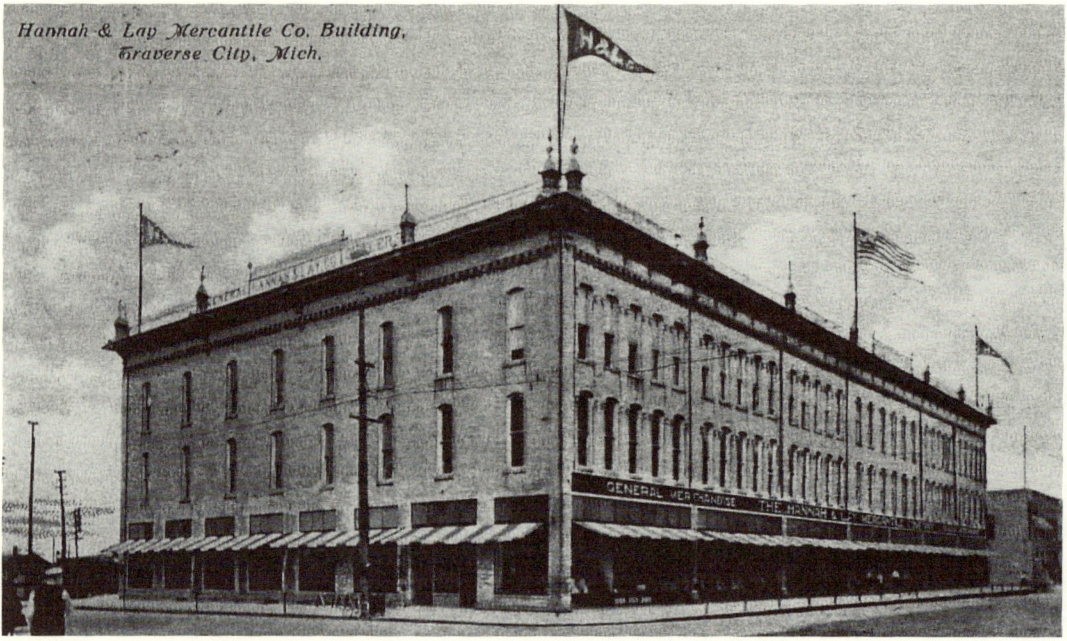
Hannah & Lay Mercantile Co. Building,
Traverse City, Mich.
GENERAL MERCHANDISE

Hannah, Lay Mercantile's "Big Store" was built in 1883.

County Jail, Traverse City, Mich.

The County Jail was built in 1884.

Tug and Schooner off Traverse City, Mich.

1886-1910

Orson Peck's first double-wide card shows TC waterfront profile around 1890.

Speed Boat Race at Traverse City, Mich.

Orson Peck may have dubbed in the boats.

18.

The *Columbia* at Bassett Island dock in 1906.

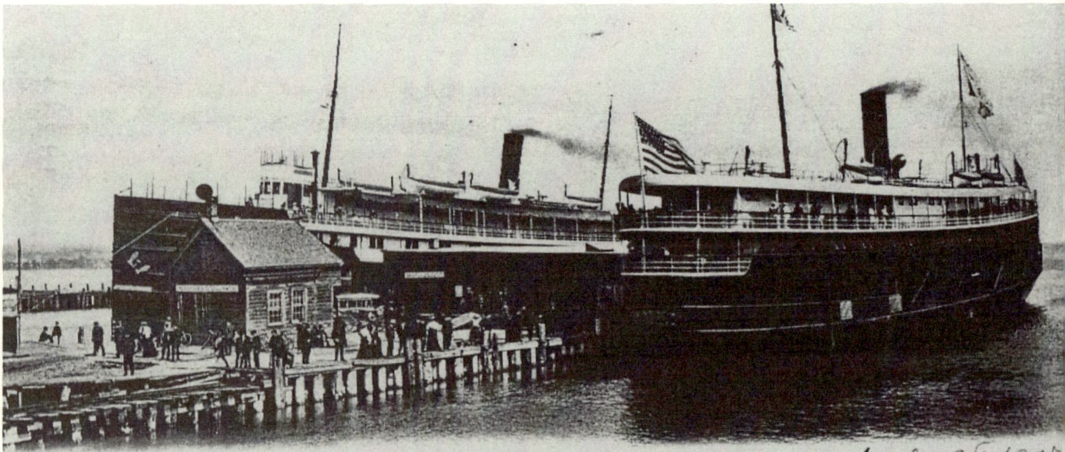

Strs. Illinois and Missouri at Dock, Traverse City, Mich. July 28. 1907.

Dear Mae, These are two of our boats which come in regularly. Aunt is sending you. Everything is lovely & the visiting is progressing in fine shape.
Anna

Missouri at N. M. T. Co's Dock, Traverse City, Mich.

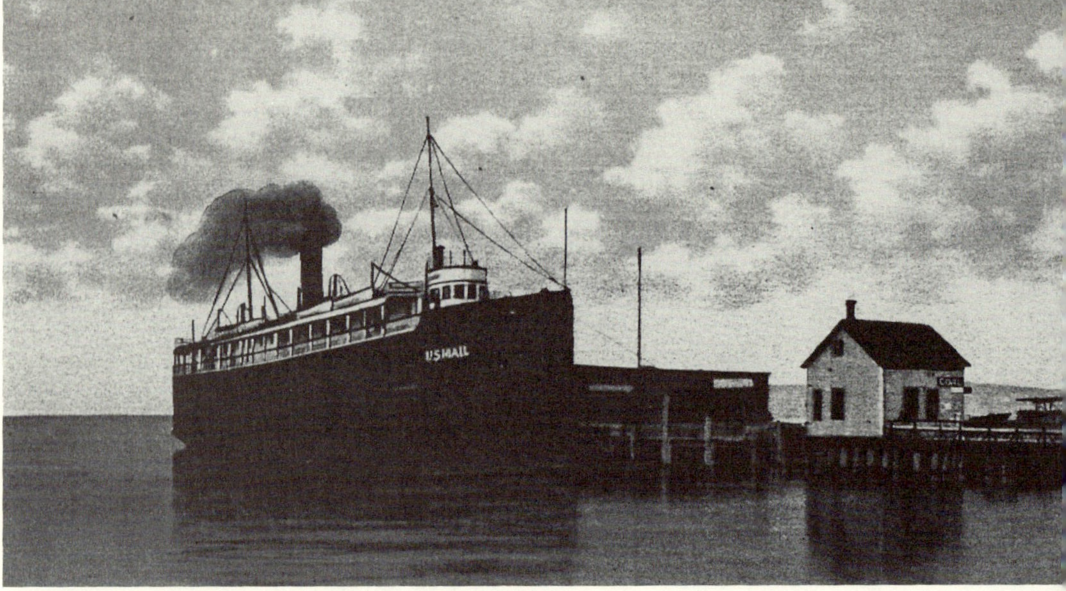

The *Missouri* and the *Chequamegon* at TC docks early 1900s.

Steamers *Illinois, Columbia* and *Lou Cummings*.

The *Roosevelt* and the *Lena Knoblock* early 1900s.

Traverse City, Leelanau and Manistique Railroad car ferry at TC docks, July 4, 1907, on excursion.

Welcoming crowd for excursionists on the Fourth of July, 1907.

The *Illinois*.

Manistique Marquette & Northern Car Ferry No. 1

TCL&M Car Ferry No. 1 plied between Northport and Manistique in early 1900s.

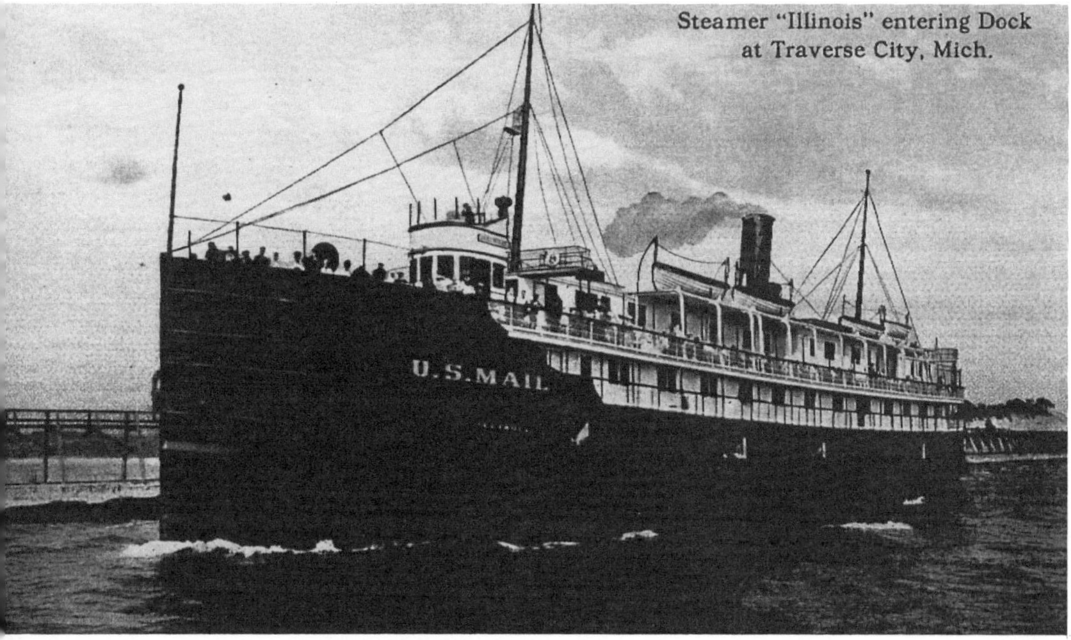
Steamer "Illinois" entering Dock
at Traverse City, Mich.
U.S.MAIL

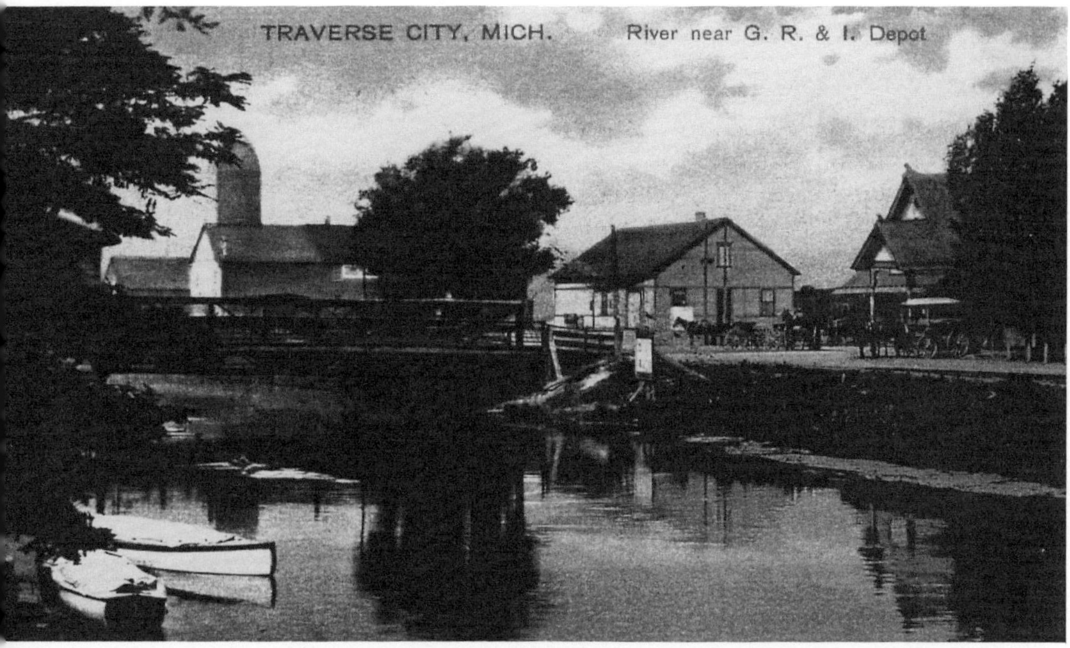
TRAVERSE CITY, MICH.
River near G. R. & I. Depot

Grand Rapids and Indiana Railroad depot at the foot of Park Street was built in 1897.

Peck's fun: police at GR&I depot.

GR&I depot, 1910.

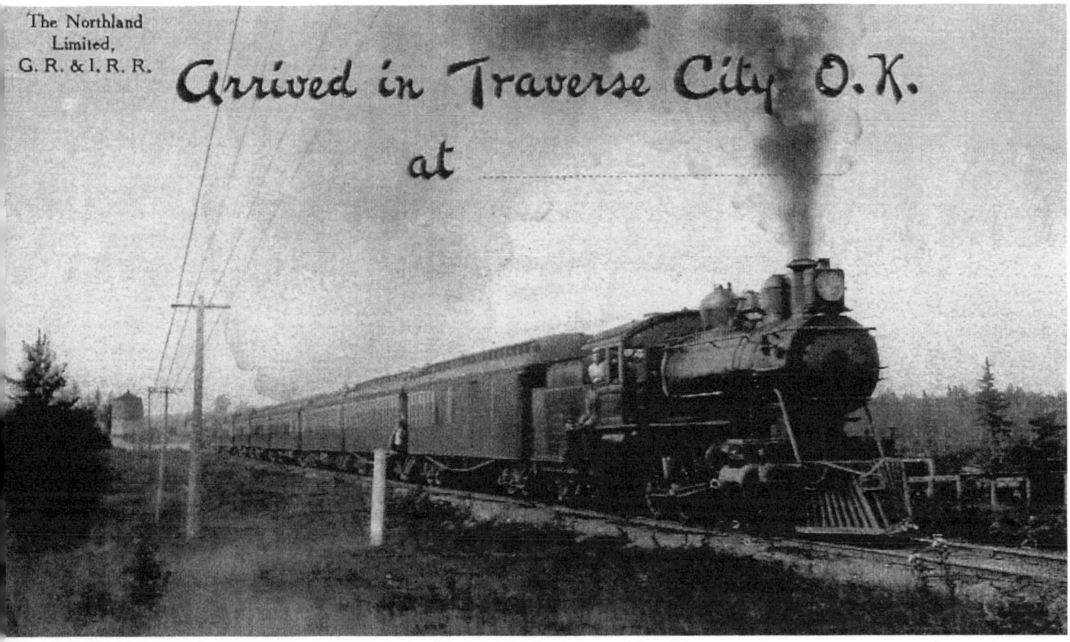
The Northland Limited, G. R. & I. R. R.
Arrived in Traverse City O.K.
at

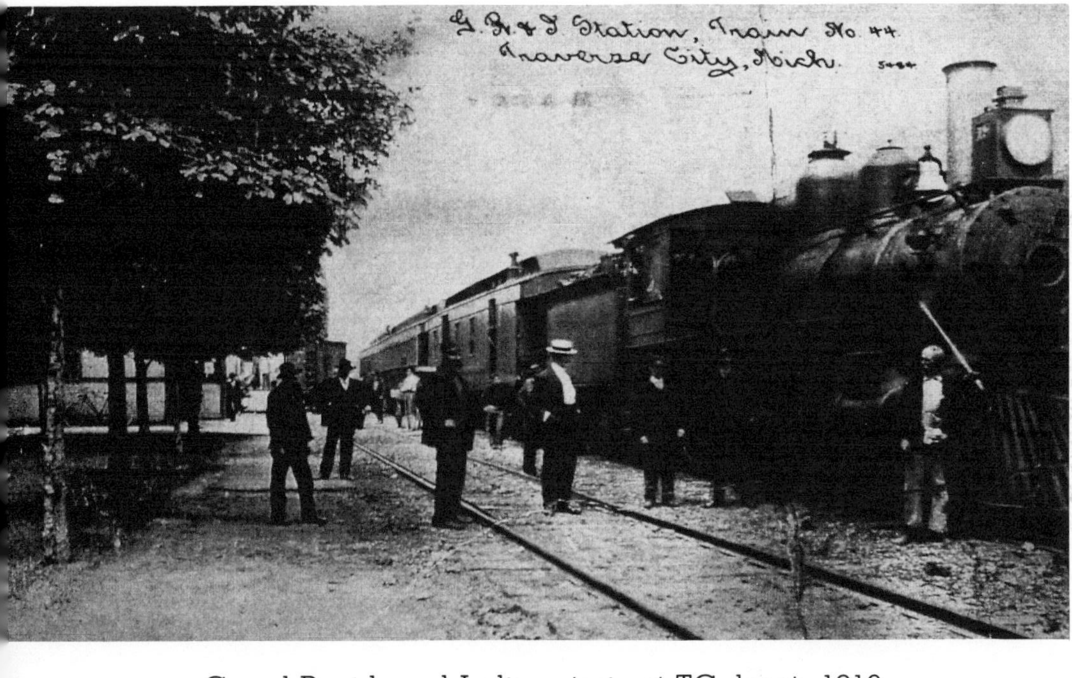
G. R. & I. Station, Train No. 44
Traverse City, Mich.
5484

Grand Rapids and Indiana train at TC depot, 1910.

GR&I passenger train on east side of Boardman Lake, 1910.

WILL WRITE MORE LATER.

NEAR WEQUETONG CLUB HOUSE,
TRAVERSE CITY, MICH.

ORSON W. PECK, PHOTO

Manistee and Northeastern Railroad depot at Union and Bay streets, 1908.

GR&I crossing near 8th and Woodmere streets, 1910.

On the TCL&M, 1907.

TCL&M plowing snow in Leelanau County.

Beitner's sawmill on Boardman Lake was built in 1897.

Mitchell sawmill on East Bay, 1890.

Oval Wood Dish factory, built in 1892, on Boardman Lake.

Williams flooring factory on Boardman Lake.

Straub & Amiotte candy factory, Traverse City Canning Co., City Gas Works, early 1900s.

The Hame Factory at the south end of Boardman Lake, around 1890.

The Starch Factory on Bay Street was built in 1899, torn down in 1922.

The candy factory was built in 1905 on the corner of Front and Hall streets.

The Wells-Higman Basket Factory was built on East 8th Street in 1892, burned down in 1950.

Copyright 1905 by the Rotograph Co.
A 7645 Lumber Mills, Traverse City, Mich.

Oval Wood Dish factory on Boardman Lake in 1905.

Milliken-Hamilton store and First National Bank, corner of Front and Cass.

Fire station on Cass Street, built in 1891.

Wilhelm building, Front and Union, built in 1900.

County courthouse was finished in 1899.

Court House and Jail, Traverse City, Mich.

E 1892 Court House, North Front, Traverse City, Mich.

JOHNSON HOSPITAL. COR. STATE AND WELLINGTON STS.. TRAVERSE CITY. MICH.

The City Opera House, built in 1892.

No. 3 Whiting Hotel, Traverse City, Mich.

The Whiting Hotel was built in 1894.

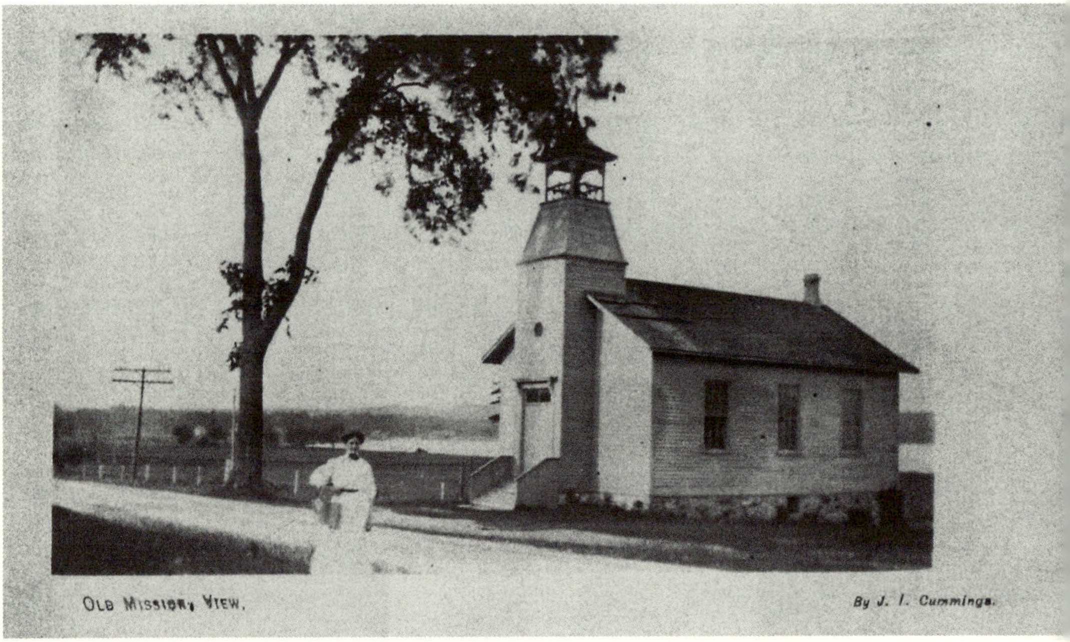

OLD MISSION, VIEW.

By J. I. Cummings.

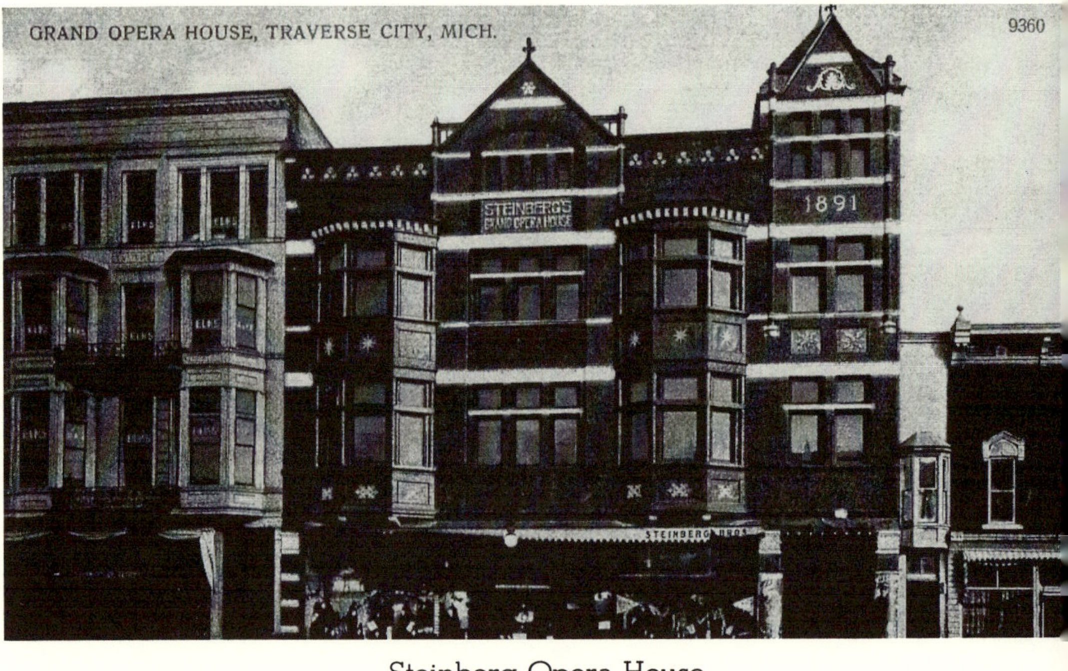

GRAND OPERA HOUSE, TRAVERSE CITY, MICH.

Steinberg Opera House

Perry Hannah finished his retirement home on Sixth Street in 1903.

Andrew Carnegie donated funds for City Library, built in 1904 on Sixth Street.

The Traverse City State Bank, built 1903-04.

The Ladies Library on Cass Street was built in 1909.

TC Post Office at Cass and State was built in 1904.

W. Cary Hull (Oval Wood Dish) built this house at
Washington and Wellington in 1905.

Spanish-American war veterans in camp, 1907.

Traverse City *Daily Eagle* building at 113 East Front.

First National Bank built in 1908.

FIRST NATIONAL BANK, TRAVERSE CITY, MICHIGAN. ANNUAL FRUIT DISPLAYS SINCE 1906 — PERMANENT GLASS EXHIBIT

St. Francis Church, 10th Street, built in 1883, torn down in 1979.

Elmwood School, built in 1892, torn down in 1956.

Central High School, built in 1886.

Oak Park School, built in 1895, torn down in 1960s.

Boardman Avenue School burned down in 1913.

Congregational Church, built in 1905.

Union Street School, built in 1893.

Central Methodist Church, built in 1912.

The First Baptist Church was built in 1874.

Union Street looking north, early 1900s.

Union Street around 1890, Hotel Shilson at left.

54.

Front Street around 1895.

Front Street looking east, 1905.

July 4, 1907 parade.

Fourth of July parade on Front Street, 1907.

Front Street parade, July 4, 1908.

Front Street looking east, 1908.

Front Street looking west, 1908.

Fourth of July parade, 1908.

Orson Peck's streetcar on Front Street, early 1900s.

Front Street looking west, around 1920.

Undertaker Will Anderson and TC Mayor "Wild Bill" Germaine in comic pose on Park Street, around 1908.

Front Street, 1920s.

Sixth Street, 1906.

Sixth Street, 1909.

61.

Dairy horse and wagon.

Front St. Bridge, Traverse City, Mich.

West Front Street bridge, built in 1910.

Hannah Park, 1910.

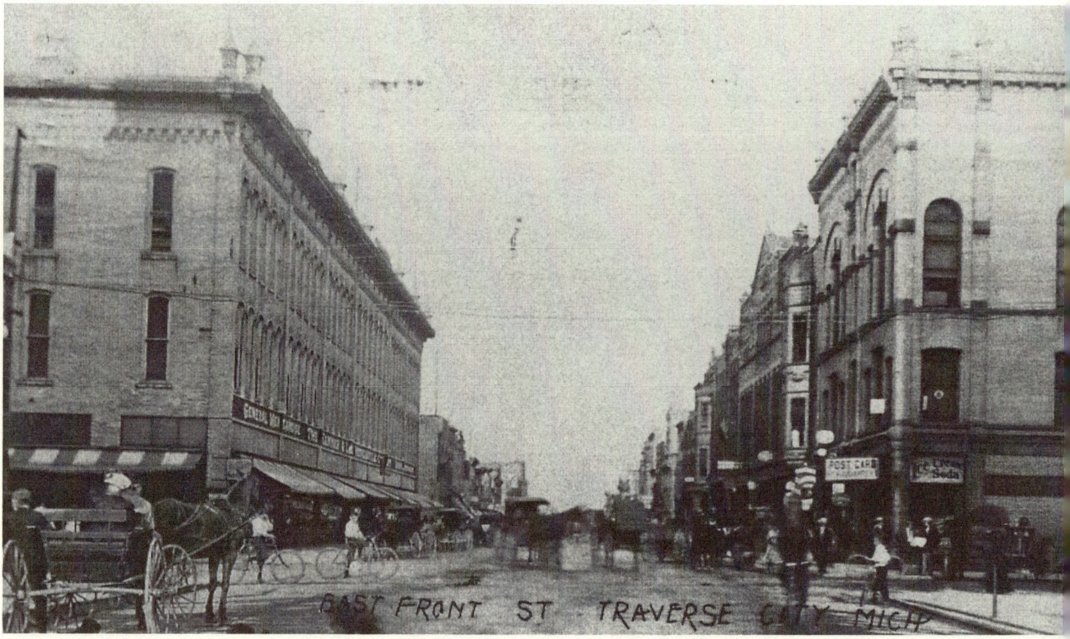
EAST FRONT ST TRAVERSE CITY MICH
POST CARD

Front Street looking east, 1910.

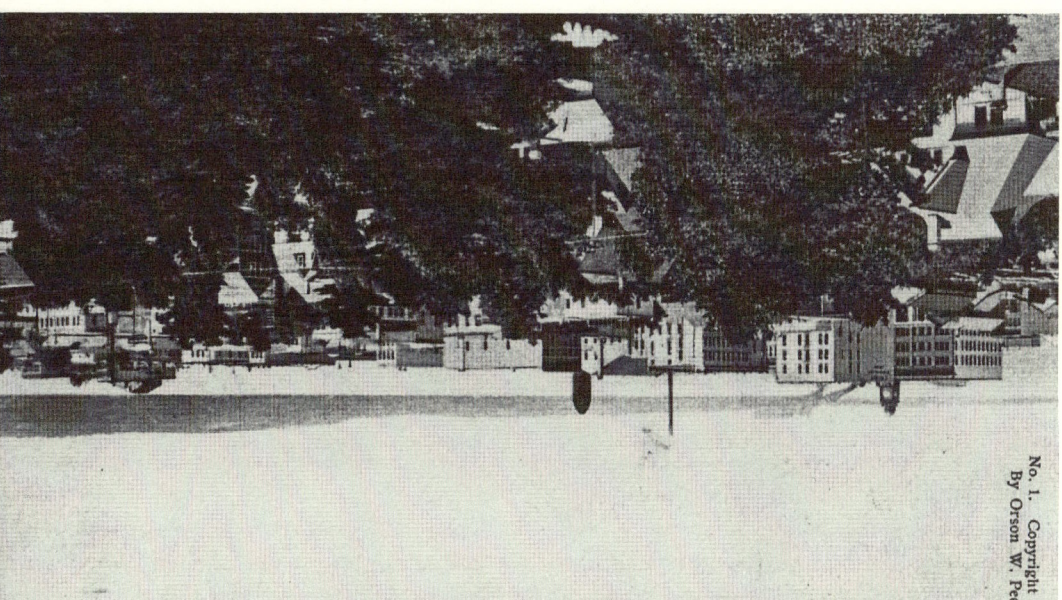

Traverse City, Mich., Business Portion.
No. 1. Copyright 1906.
By Orson W. Peck.

Cass Street looking south, 1910.

Sixth Street looking west, 1910.

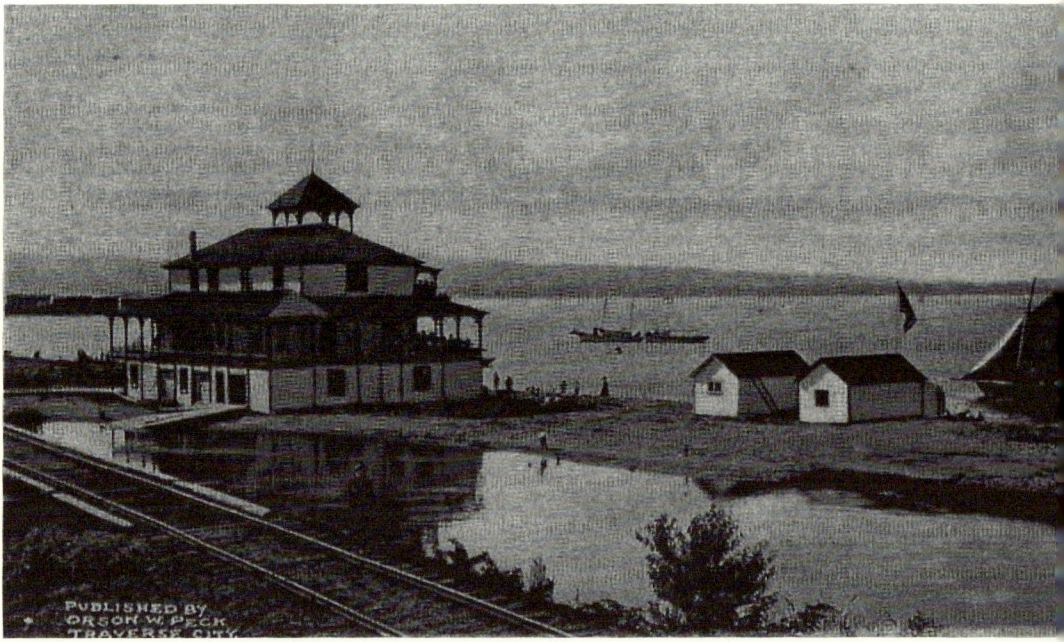
PUBLISHED BY
ORSON W. PECK
TRAVERSE CITY

Wequetong clubhouse was built in 1894.

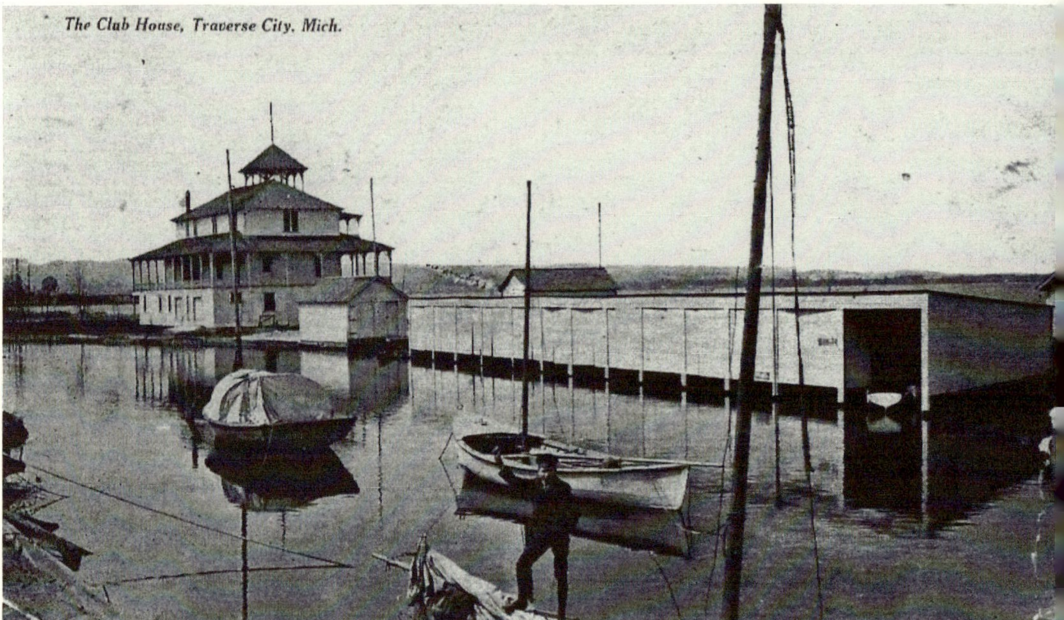
The Club House, Traverse City, Mich.

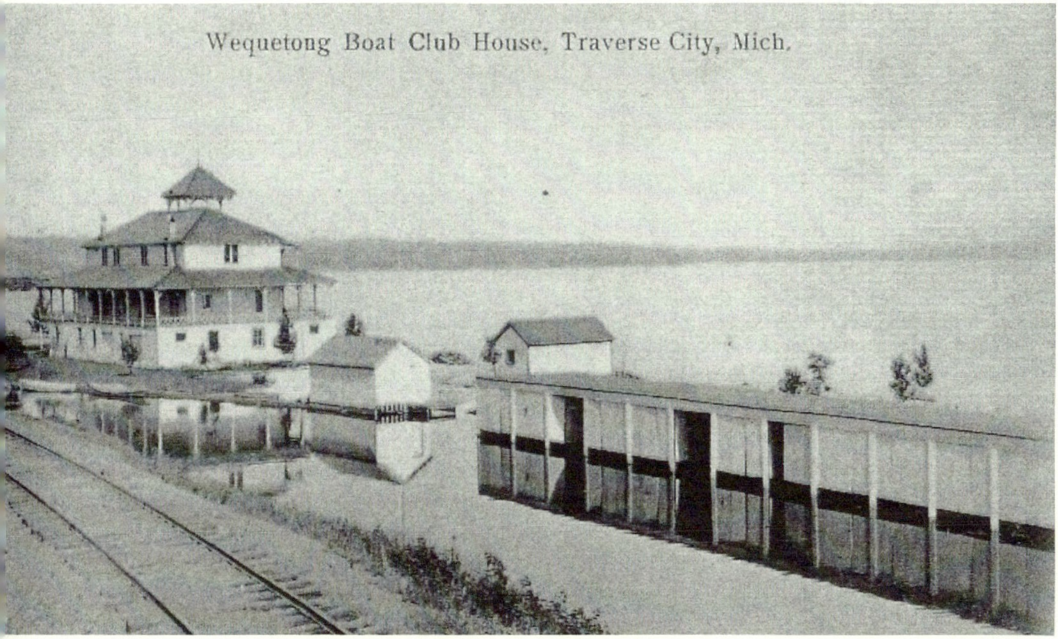
Wequetong Boat Club House, Traverse City, Mich.

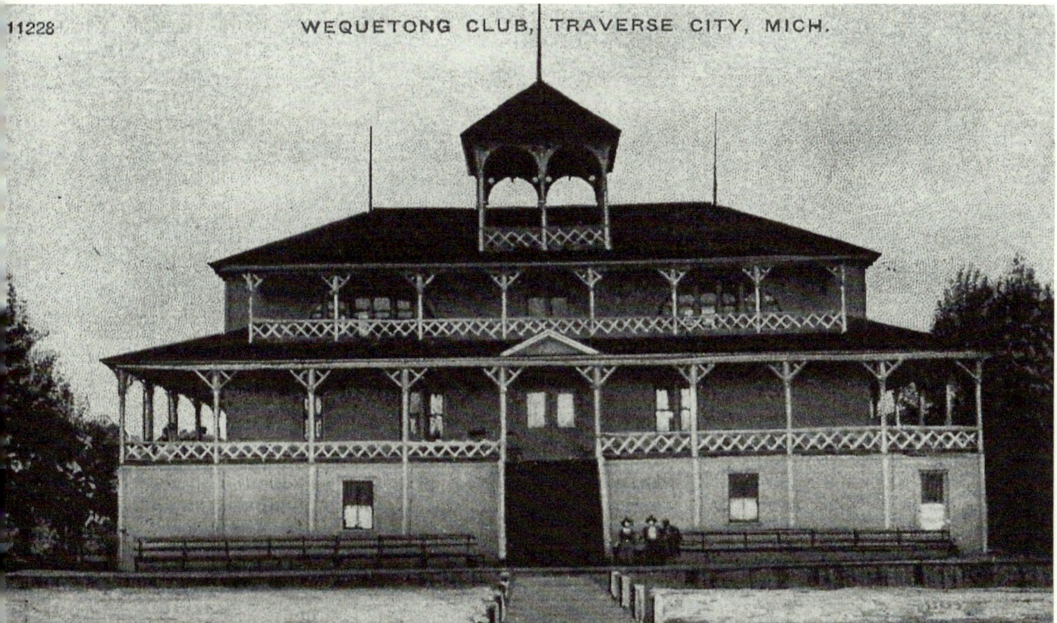
11228
WEQUETONG CLUB, TRAVERSE CITY, MICH.

Edgewood Resort beach on east side of West Bay.

68.

Waterfront in 1905.

Deer enclosure at Hannah Park, early 1900s.

Marion Island dock, 1904. (Actually Bassett Island)

WHAT HAS BECOME OF YOU
Why don't you write ?

Marion Island was renamed Ford Island in 1918.

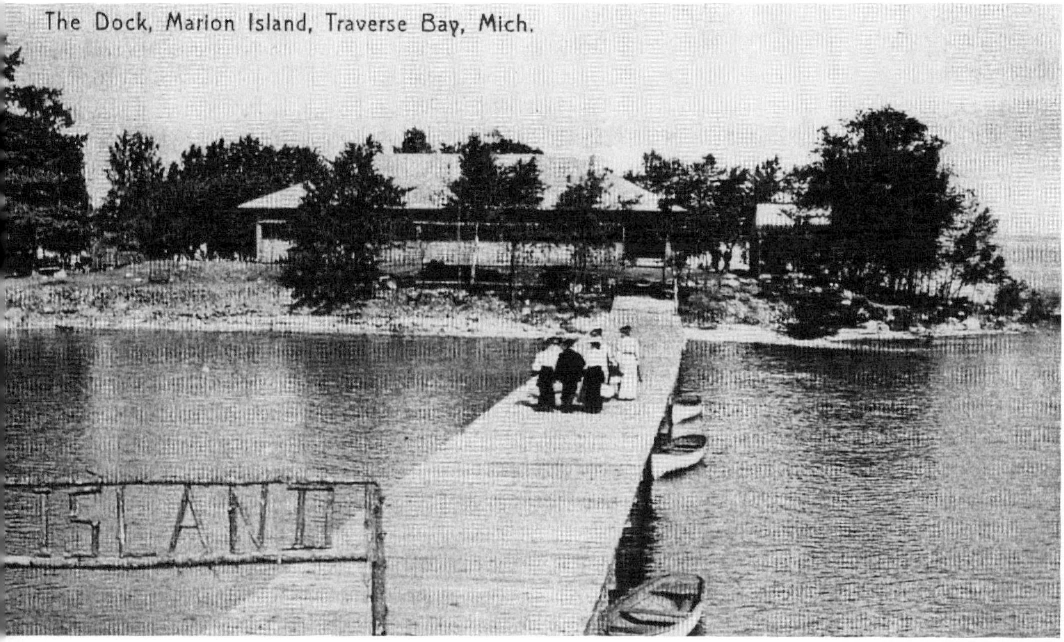
The Dock, Marion Island, Traverse Bay, Mich.
ISLAND

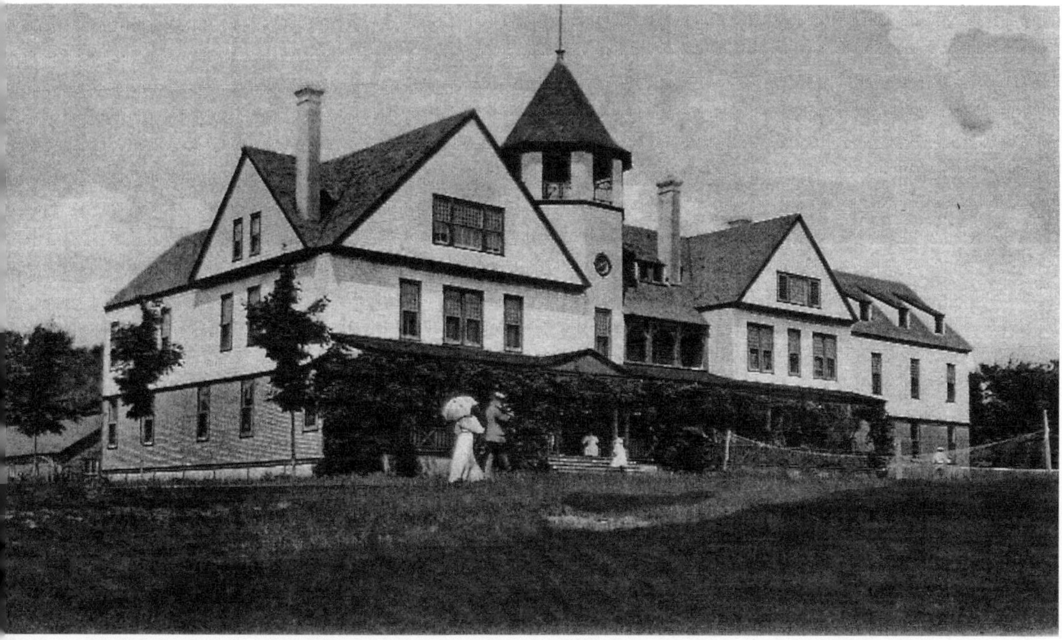

Neahtawanta Resort, near Bowers Harbor on Old Mission peninsula.

72.

OLD MISSION, VIEW.   By J. I. Cummings.

COTTAGES AT EDGEWOOD, TRAVERSE CITY, MICH.

Birchwood Resort on West Bay, 1907.

Boardman Lake, 1910.

74.

Iceboats on Bay, Wequetong Club in background, 1910.

East Front street.

Candy factory's float in 1908 parade.

1st Prize Float, July 4th, Traverse City, Mich.

76.

Bathing beauty, 1909.

1911-1930

Washington Street, looking east, 1912.

78.

Washington Street, looking West, Traverse City, Mich.

APPLE AND PRODUCE SHOW HELD AT TRAVERSE CITY STATE BANK. NOVEMBER 9-16, 191

The water hole at Cass Street bridge.

Corner of 8th Street and Pine.

80.

Sixth Street, 1911.

Sixth Street, 1911.

Cass Street bridge, looking west, 1913.

Hannah Park, 1911.

Eighth Street, 1914.

83.

Front Street, looking east, 1920s.

East Front Street, 1920s.

84.

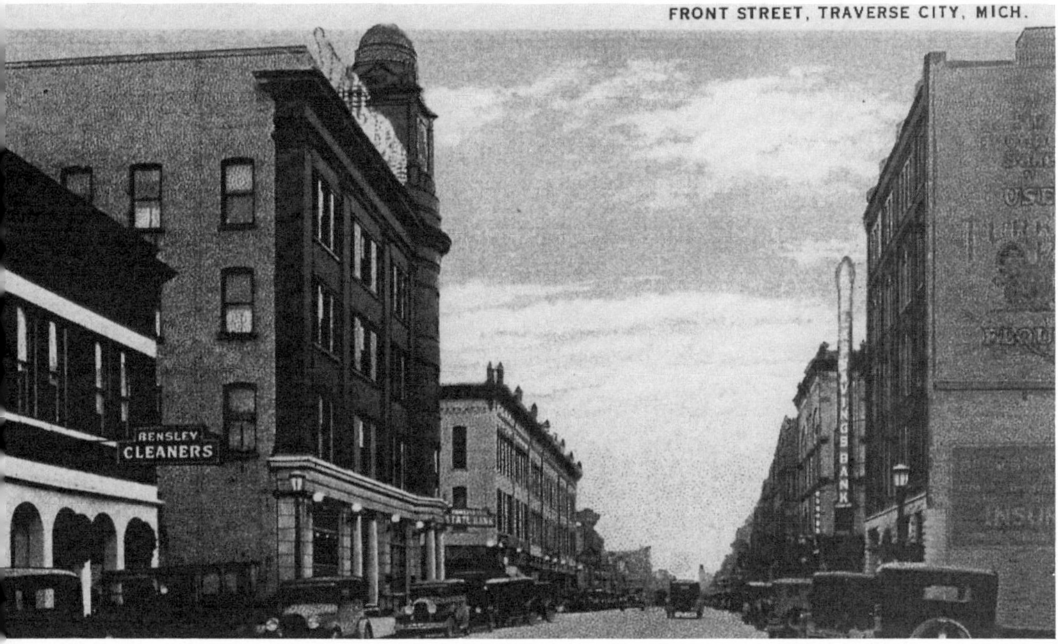
FRONT STREET, TRAVERSE CITY, MICH.
BENSLEY
CLEANERS
SAVINGS BANK

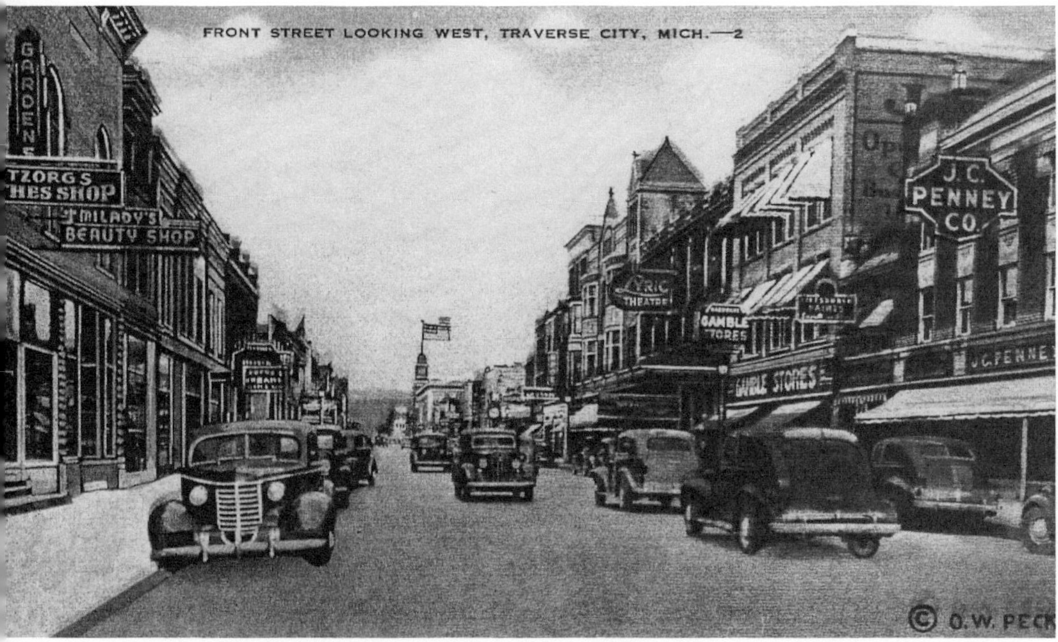
FRONT STREET LOOKING WEST, TRAVERSE CITY, MICH.—2
GARDENS
TZORGS
HES SHOP
MILADY'S
BEAUTY SHOP
LYRIC
THEATRE
GAMBLE
STORES
GAMBLE STORES
J. C.
PENNEY
CO.
J.C.PENNEY
© O.W. PECK

Front Street, looking east, 1928.

98.

Sherman & Hunter was at 205-207 East Front.

Fountain on Cass Street, built 1926, torn down 1954.

Sherman & Hunter interior.

Old Settlers headquarters on Cass Street, northwest side of bridge.

Waterworks, Traverse City, Mich.

Orson Peck's fantasy depot.

The hospital on M-72 just uphill from West Bay, early 1900s.

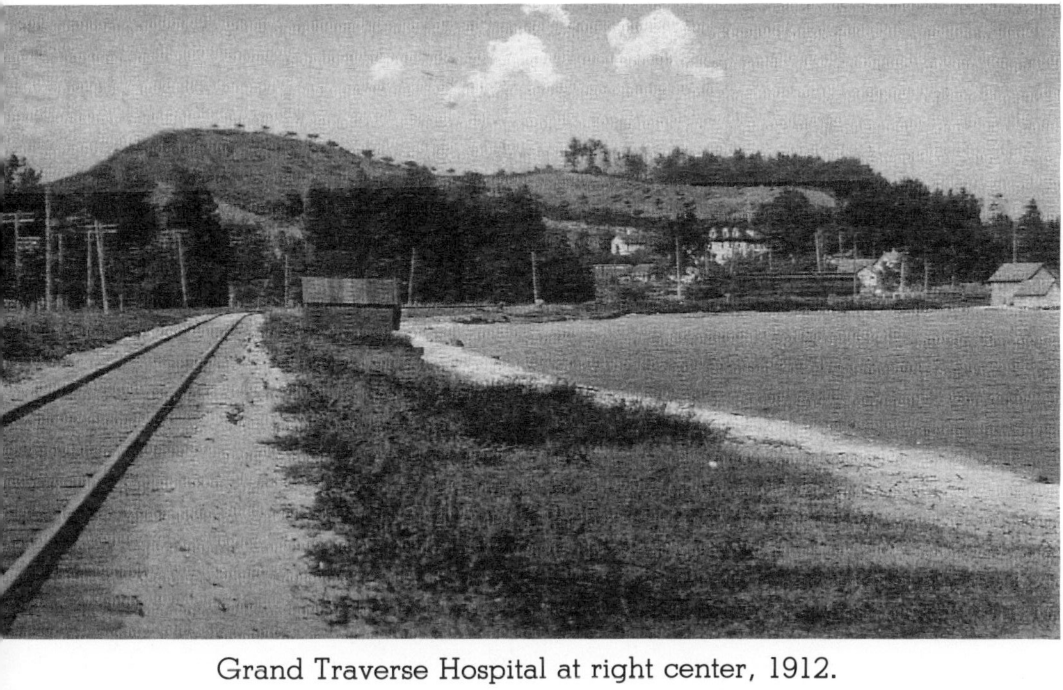

Grand Traverse Hospital at right center, 1912.

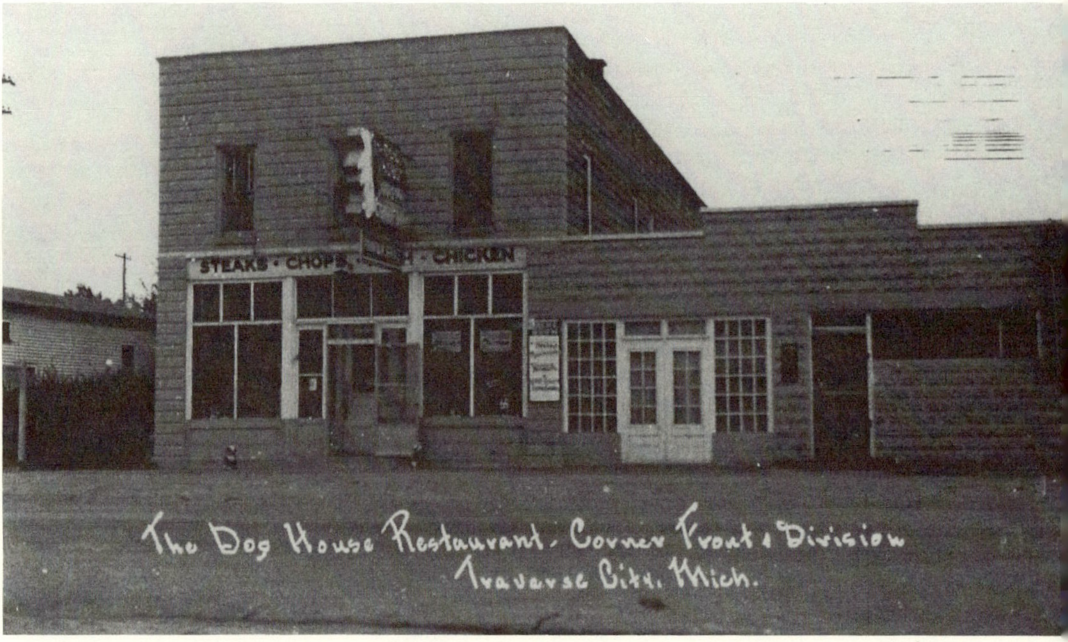
STEAKS · CHOPS
CHICKEN
The Dog House Restaurant. Corner Front & Division
Traverse City, Mich.

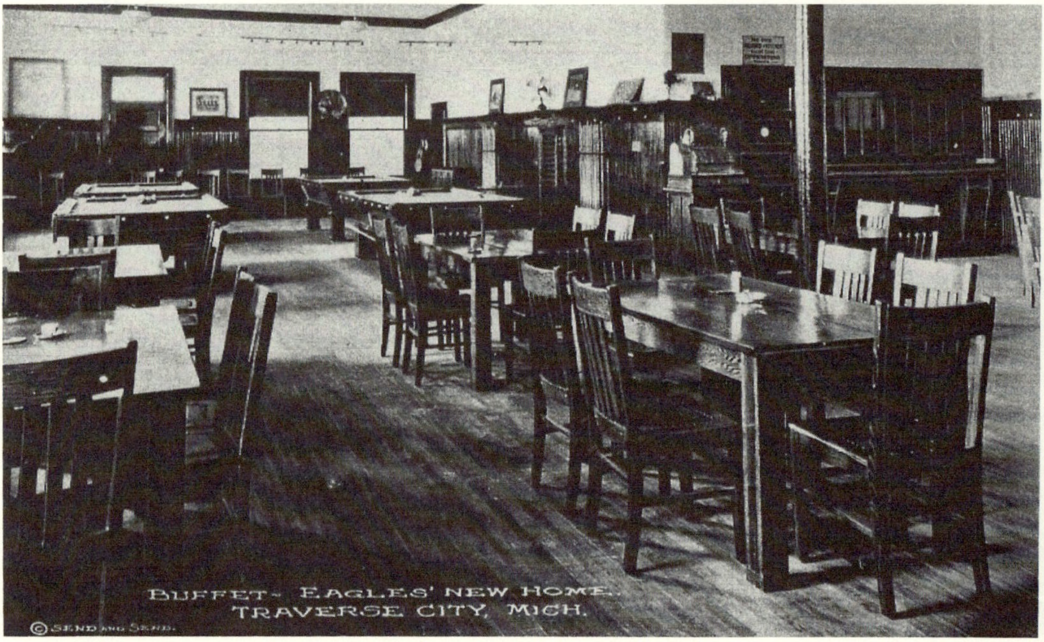
BUFFET - EAGLES' NEW HOME.
TRAVERSE CITY, MICH.
© SEND AND SEND.

Built in 1915 at 118 West Front.

B. F. Lardie's Lena Knoblock at Bowers Harbor.

94.

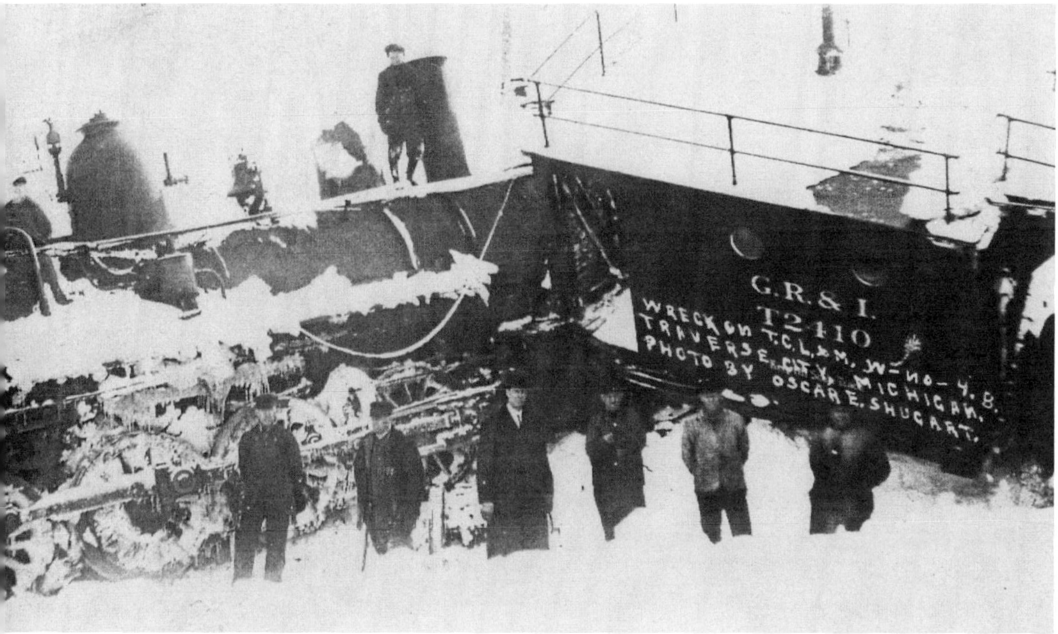

1918 photo.

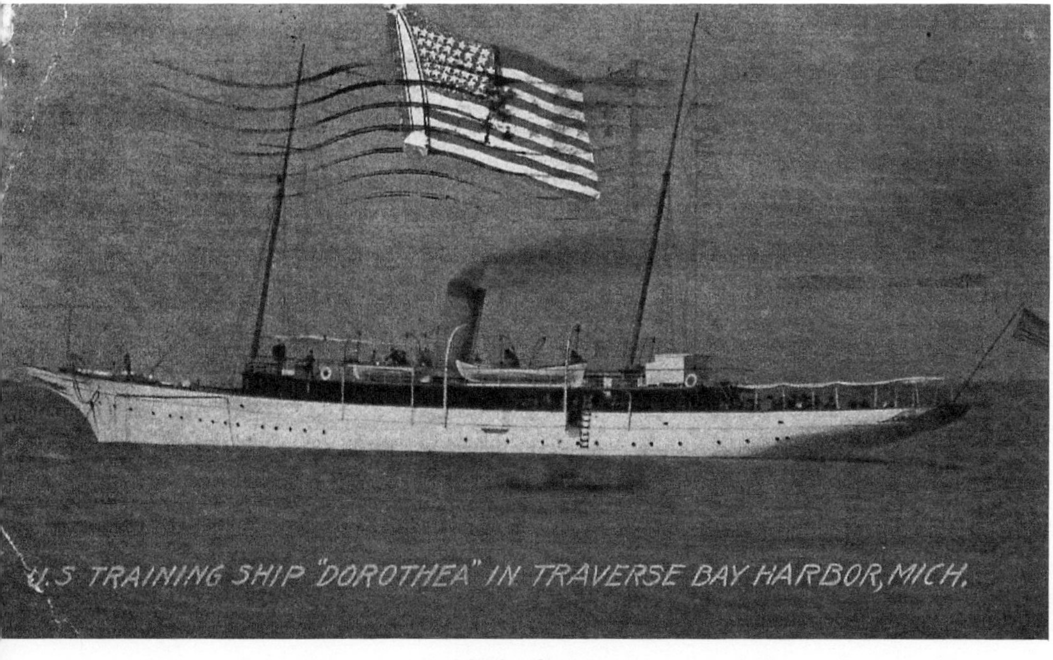

Excursion ship *Alabama*.

Excursion ship *North American* at Greilickville dock.

Early summer resort on West Bay.

Resort hotel Wisteria.

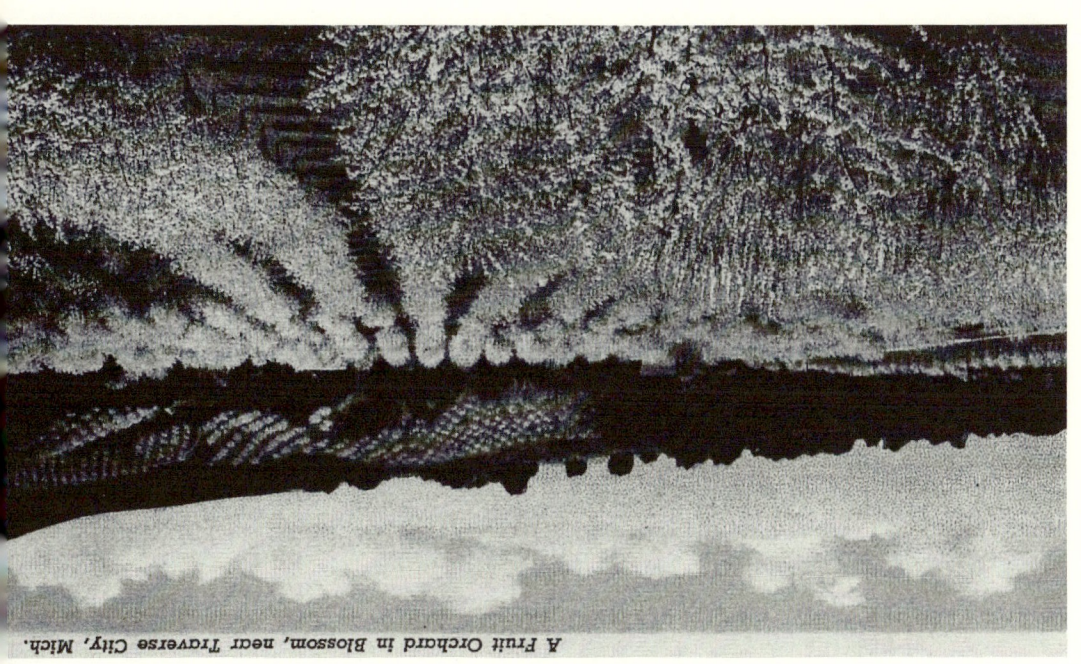

A Fruit Orchard in Blossom, near Traverse City, Mich.

Hotel Leelanau, Omena, Traverse Bay, Mich.

$4,900.00 for these Apples

This fall the apples in the Montague orchard, Grand Traverse County, were sold on the trees for $4,900. The only work that the grower had to perform in the harvesting and marketing operation, was to count the money and haul the barrels.

COMPLIMENTS OF THE TRAVERSE CITY BOARD OF TRADE

LOADS OF CHERRIES LEAVING THE MORGAN ORCHARD, TRAVERSE CITY, MICH.—33

On M-72, 1920s.

FROM PHOTO OF STRAWBERRY PATCH ON ROSE BUD FRUIT FARM. BEN BARNES, PROPRIETOR, TRAVERSE CITY, MICH., R. F. D. NO. 6. PLANTS FOR SALE. CORRESPONDENCE SOLICITED

CHERRY PICKING TIME, GRAND TRAVERSE REGION, MICH.—16

Orson Peck's huge melons.

Fanny M. Rose loading potatoes at Bowers Harbor.

BOARDMAN RIVER FROM 8TH STREET BRIDGE, TRAVERSE CITY, MICH.

1916 photo.

1911 photo.

Bathing Beach, Traverse City, Mich.

102.

Daredevil walks tightrope across Front Street in 1915.

1914 photo.

Lower Power House, Boardman River

Traverse City's famous trout fisherman.

ART WINNIE ALONG THE BOARDMAN RIVER

Traverse City Municipal Dam
Mayfield, Mich.
Sept. 17, 1921.

HANNAH PARK FROM BRIDGE, TRAVERSE CITY, MICH.   44380

1931-1950

40:—Cass St. Bridge, Hotel Park Place in the Distance, Traverse City, Mich.

H 9878 **Boardman River and Library, Traverse City, Mich.**

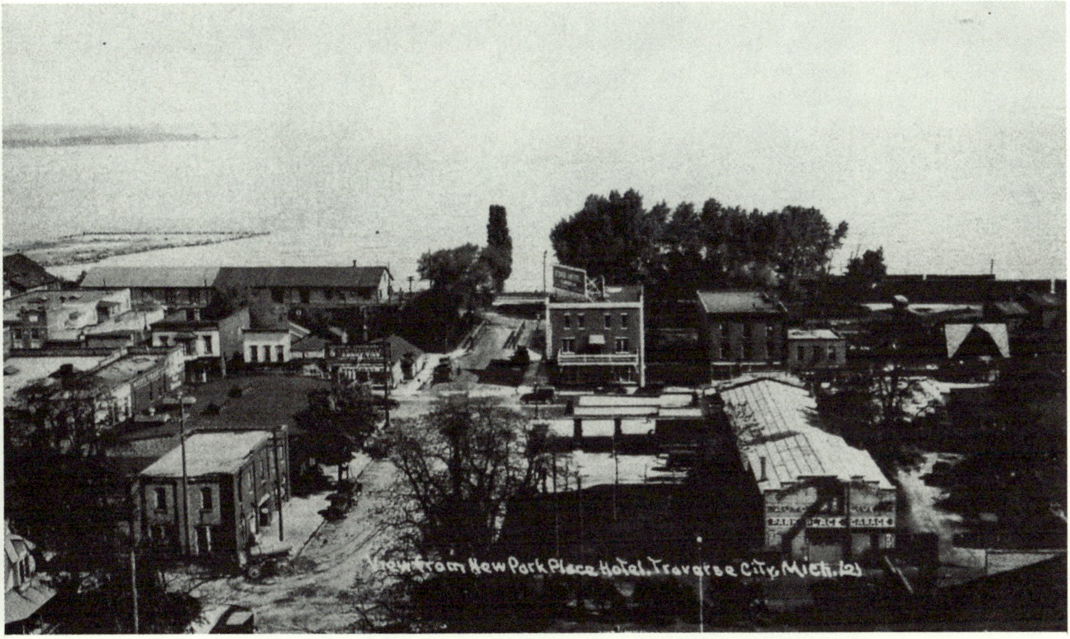
View from New Park Place Hotel, Traverse City, Mich. 121

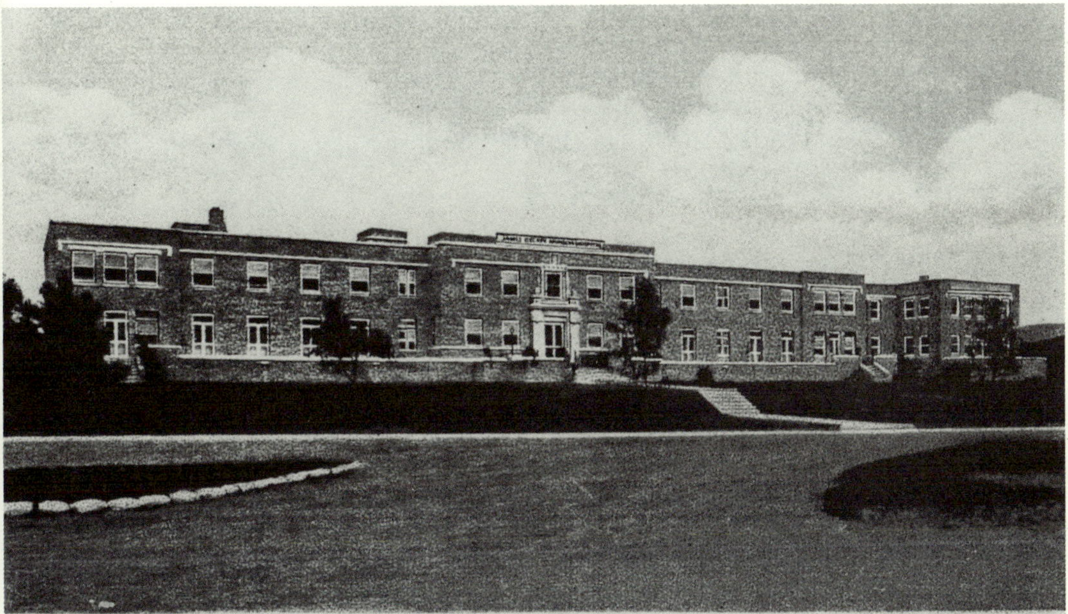

JAMES DECKER MUNSON HOSPITAL, TRAVERSE CITY, MICH. 115336

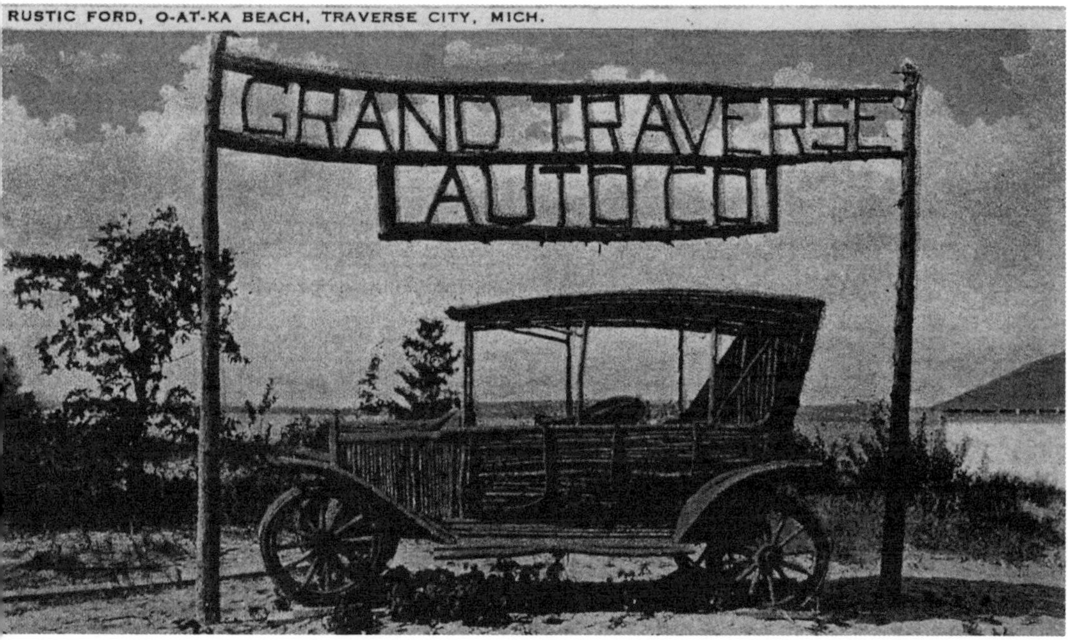
RUSTIC FORD, O-AT-KA BEACH, TRAVERSE CITY, MICH.
GRAND TRAVERSE
AUTO CO

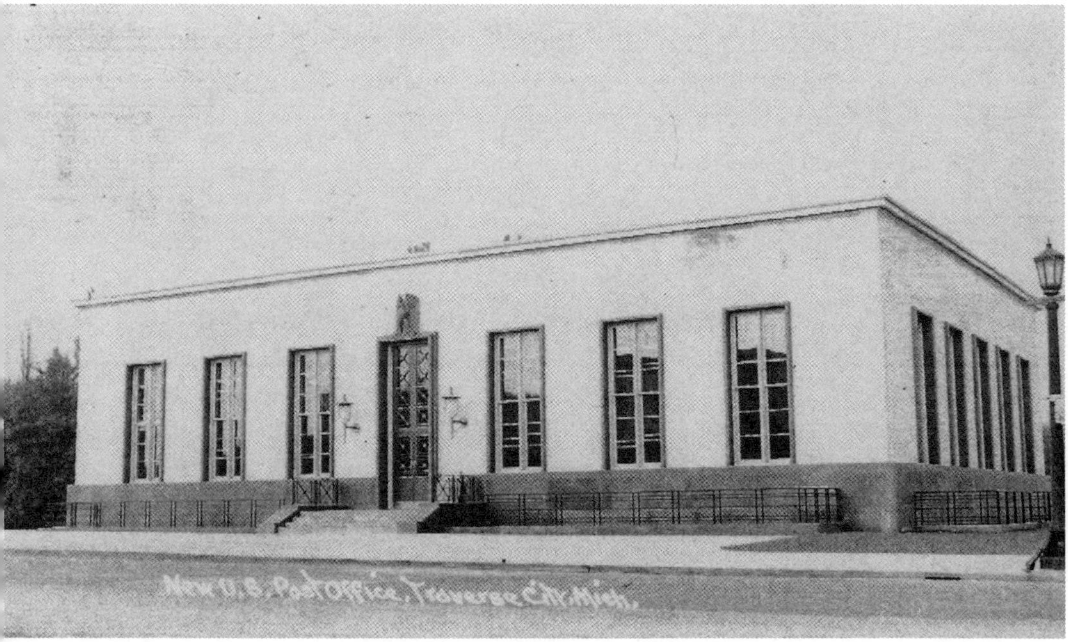
New U.S. Post Office, Traverse City, Mich.

New Post Office built in 1939.

Southwest corner of Front and Cass.

Entering Traverse City, Mich. from the South. W.S.3.

BIRCHES ALONG THE PENINSULA ROAD, TRAVERSE CITY, MICH.
© ORSON W. PECK

SENIOR HIGH SCHOOL,
TRAVERSE CITY, MICH.—9

Dr. Holdsworth's Residence, Traverse City, Mich.

At 11th and Union.

Wolverine Cafe, 150 E. Front.

At 510 East 8th Street.

GOLF AND COUNTRY CLUB, TRAVERSE CITY, MICH.

Replica of first school and church at Old Mission.

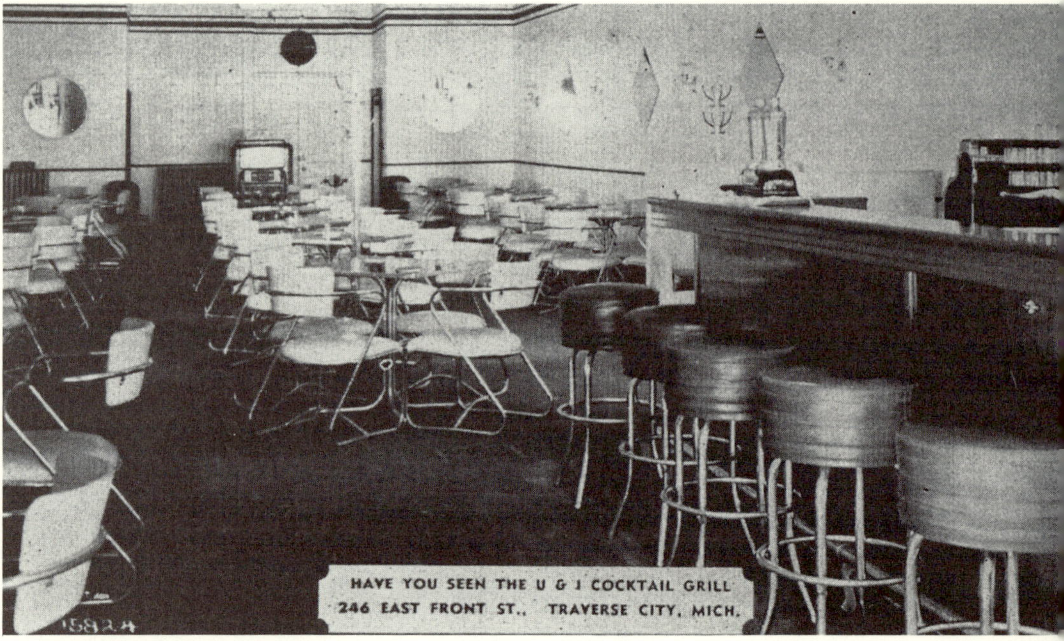
HAVE YOU SEEN THE U & I COCKTAIL GRILL
246 EAST FRONT ST., TRAVERSE CITY, MICH.

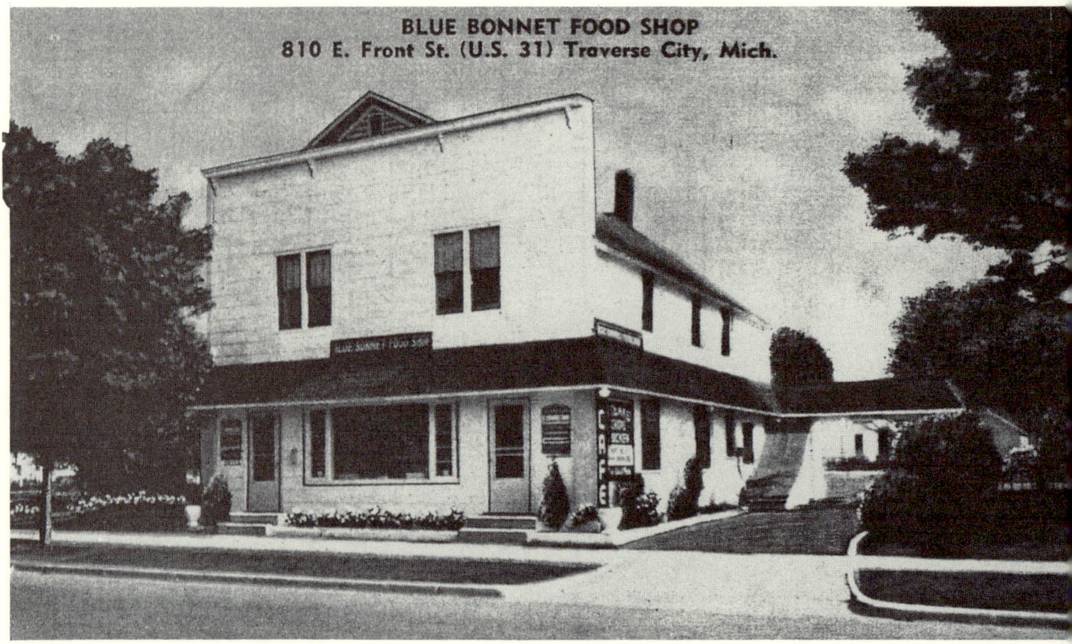
BLUE BONNET FOOD SHOP
810 E. Front St. (U.S. 31) Traverse City, Mich.
CAFE

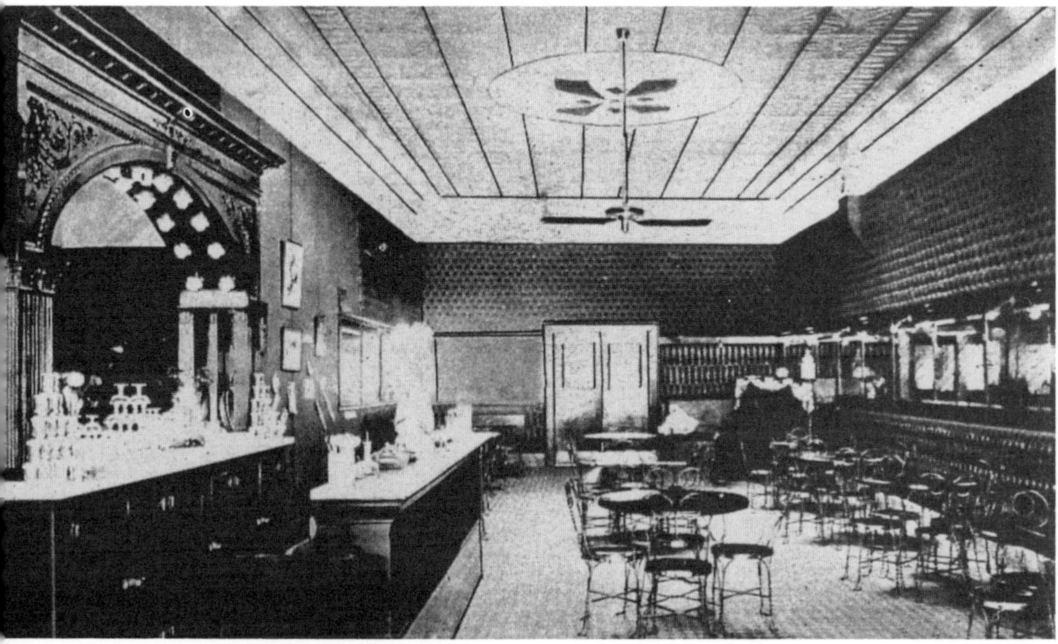

In the Palace Theater, 128 East Front Street.

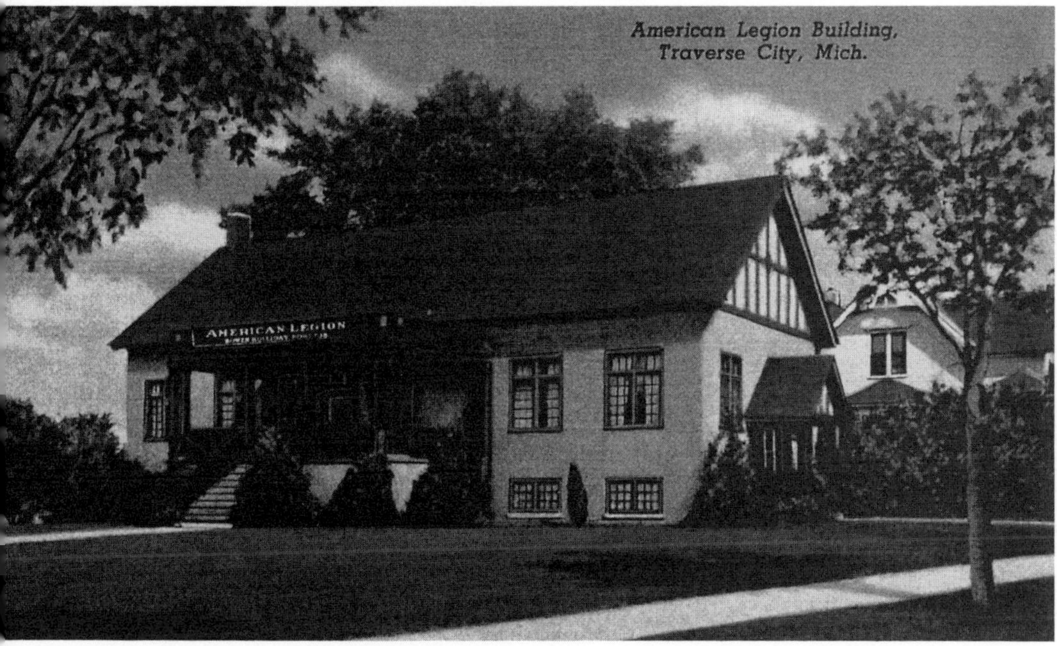
American Legion Building,
Traverse City, Mich.
AMERICAN LEGION

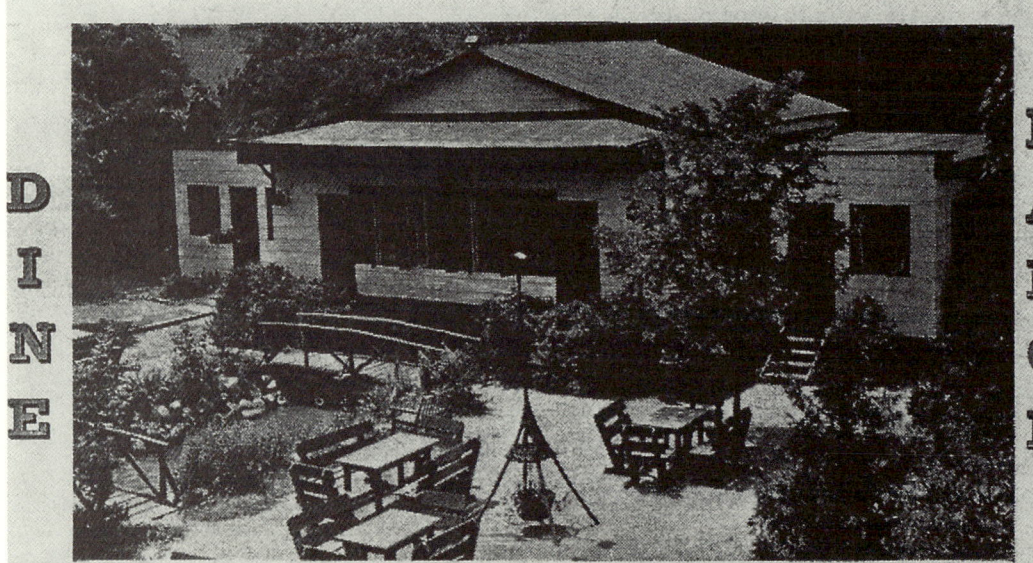

DINE
DANCE
THE BROOK Nite Club - Traverse City, Mich.

Popular nightclub on Kids Creek at N. Maple and Second Street.

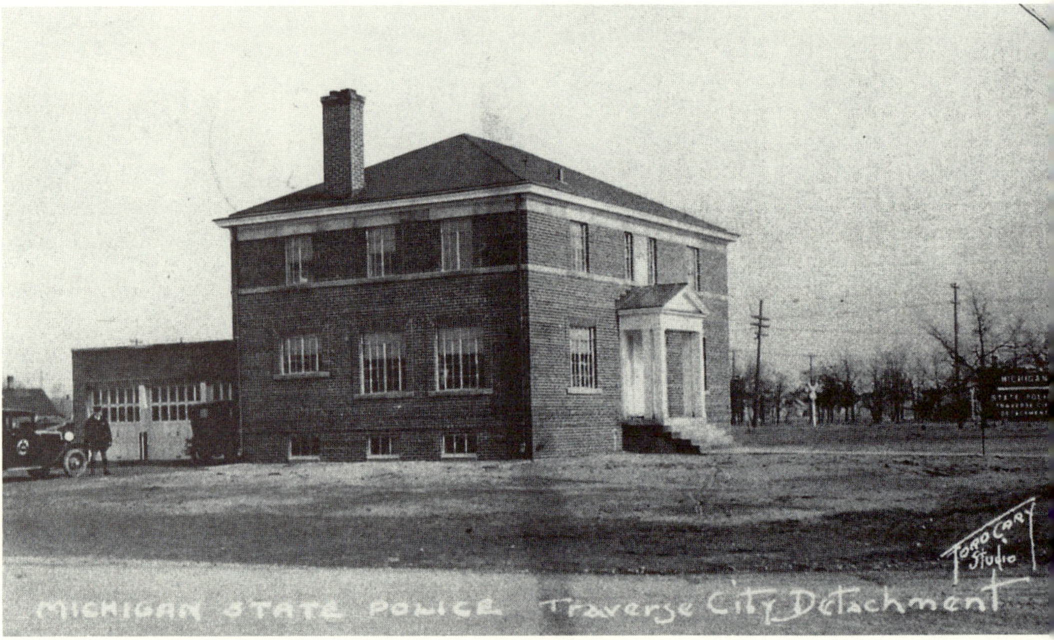
MICHIGAN STATE POLICE Traverse City Detachment

Built in 1932.

Built in 1921.

Orson Peck's fanciful photo of Charlie Augustine's flight on October 1909.

TC's first airport, on Rennie Hill, 1930s.

THE MORGAN CHERRY ORCHARD IN BLOSSOM, TRAVERSE CITY, MICH.—17

Harvest Time in a Cherry Orchard, Grand Traverse Region, Mich.

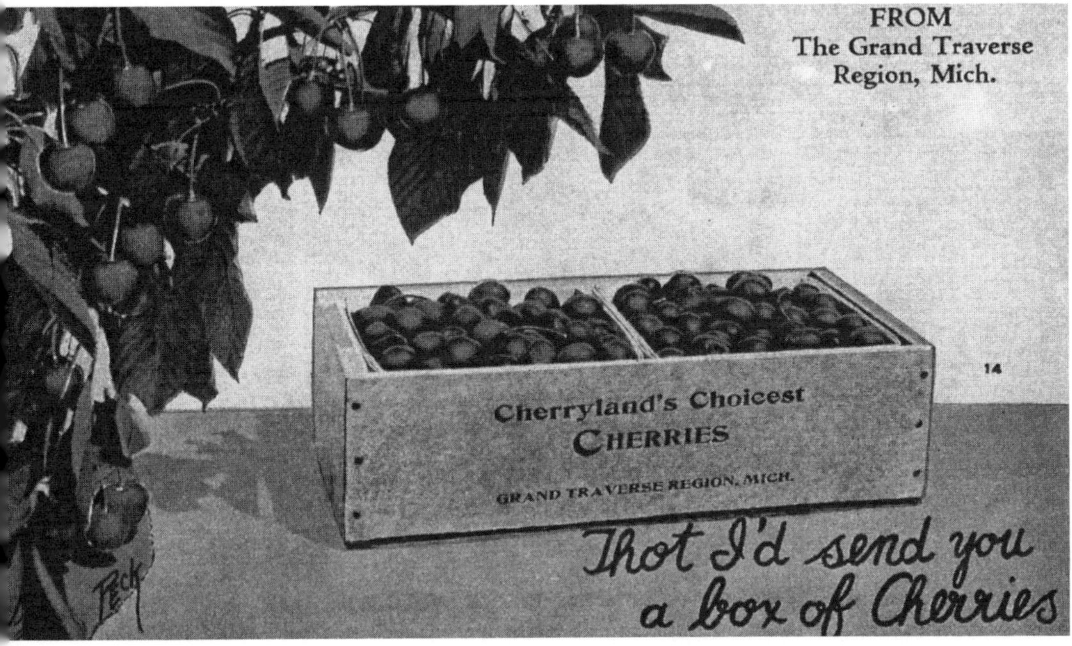
FROM
The Grand Traverse
Region, Mich.
14
Cherryland's Choicest
CHERRIES
GRAND TRAVERSE REGION, MICH.
Thot I'd send you
a box of Cherries
PECK

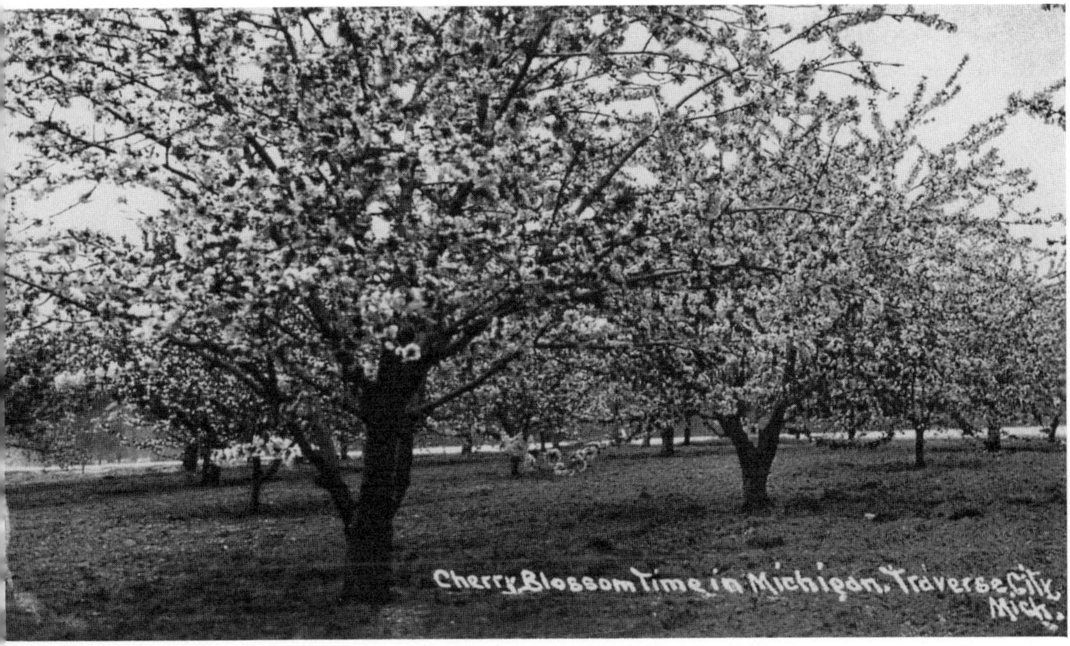
Cherry Blossom Time in Michigan, Traverse City, Mich.

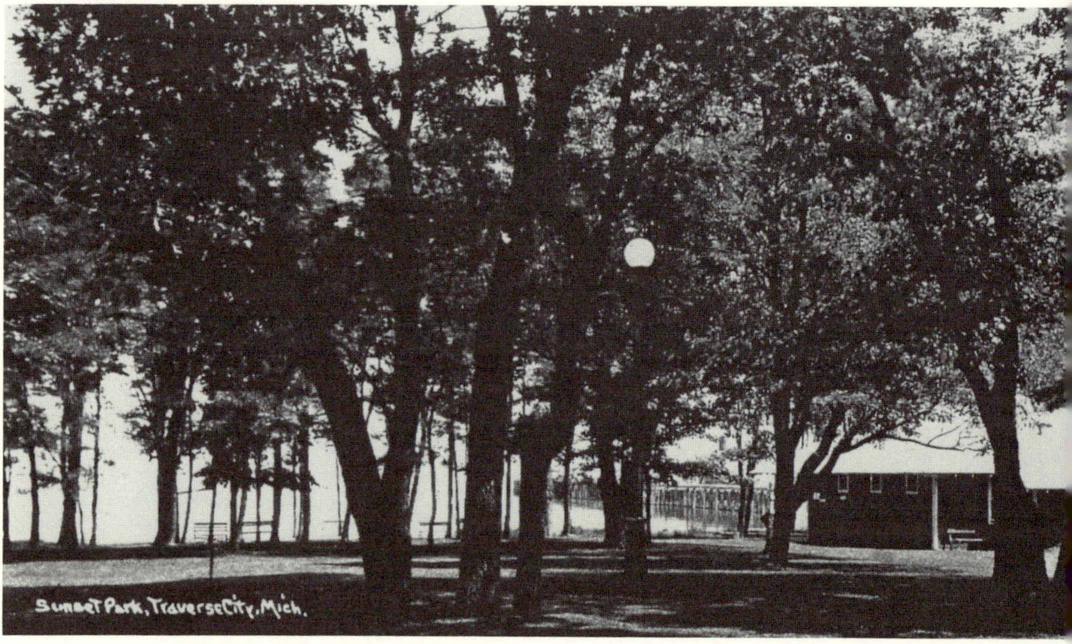

Sunset Park, Traverse City, Mich.

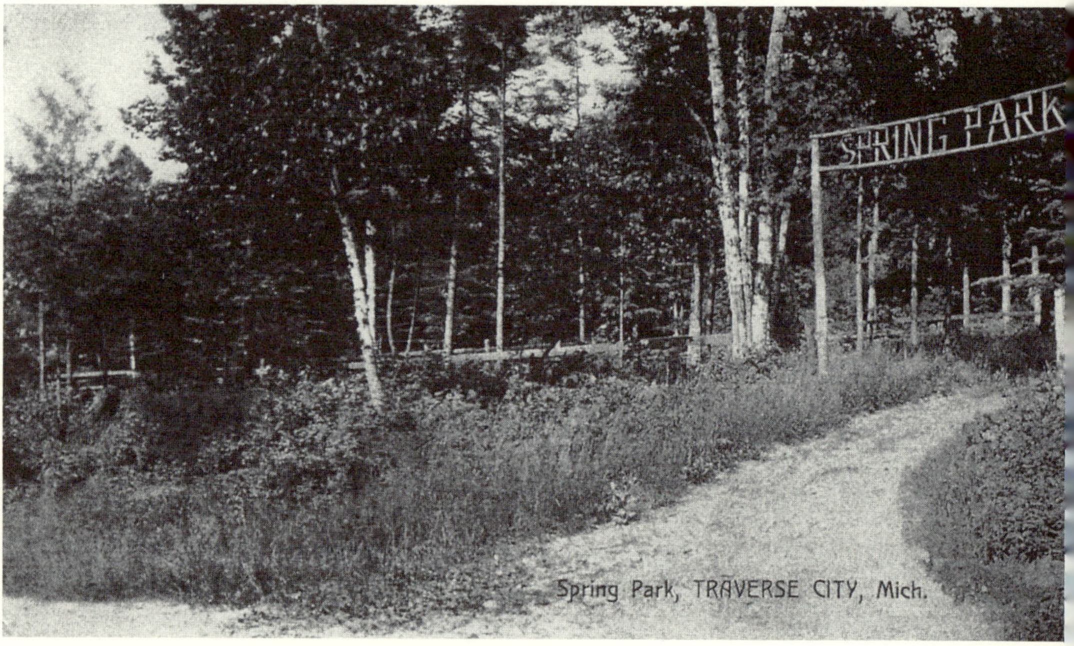

Spring Park, TRAVERSE CITY, Mich.

1921 photo.

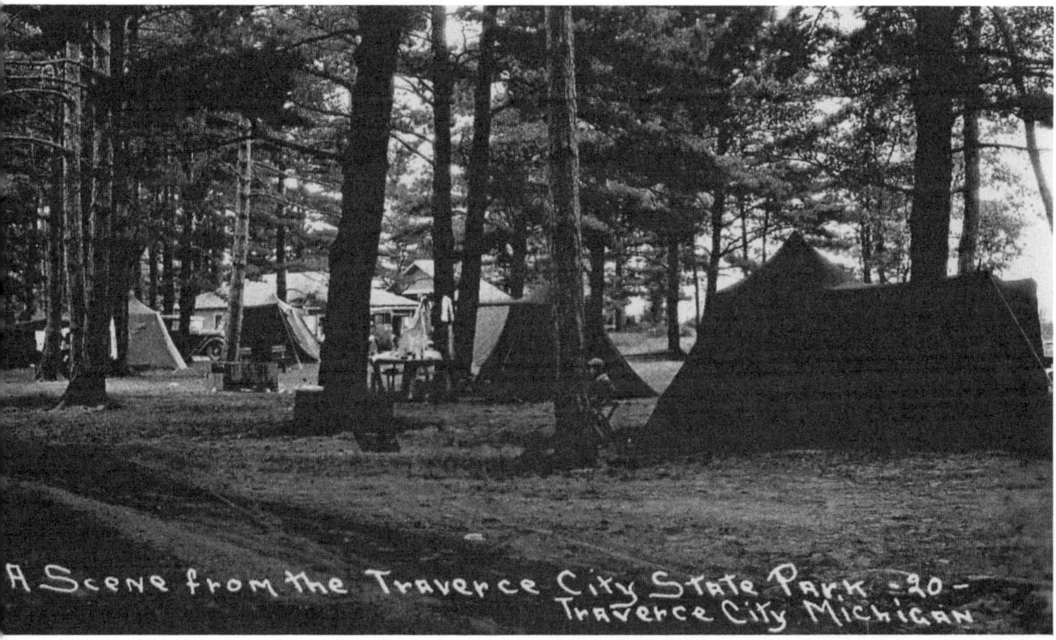

A Scene from the Traverce City State Park -20- Traverce City Michigan

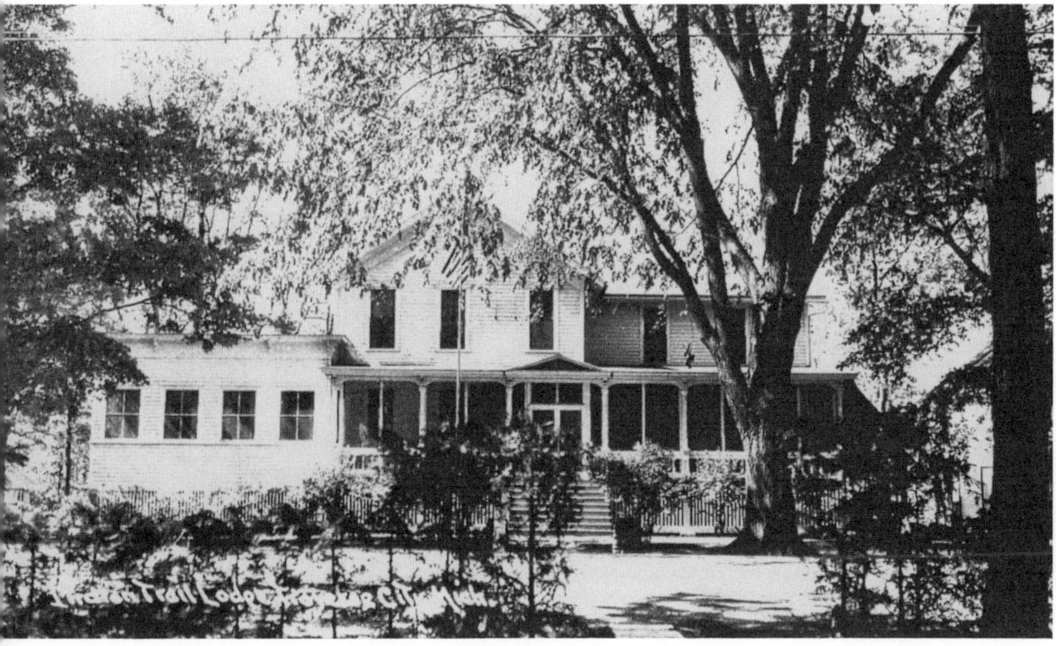

Indian Trail Lodge on US-31, East Bay.

125.

INDIAN TRAIL CAMP
TRAVERSE CITY MICH.

Indian Trail Cabins and 91 Traverse City Mich.

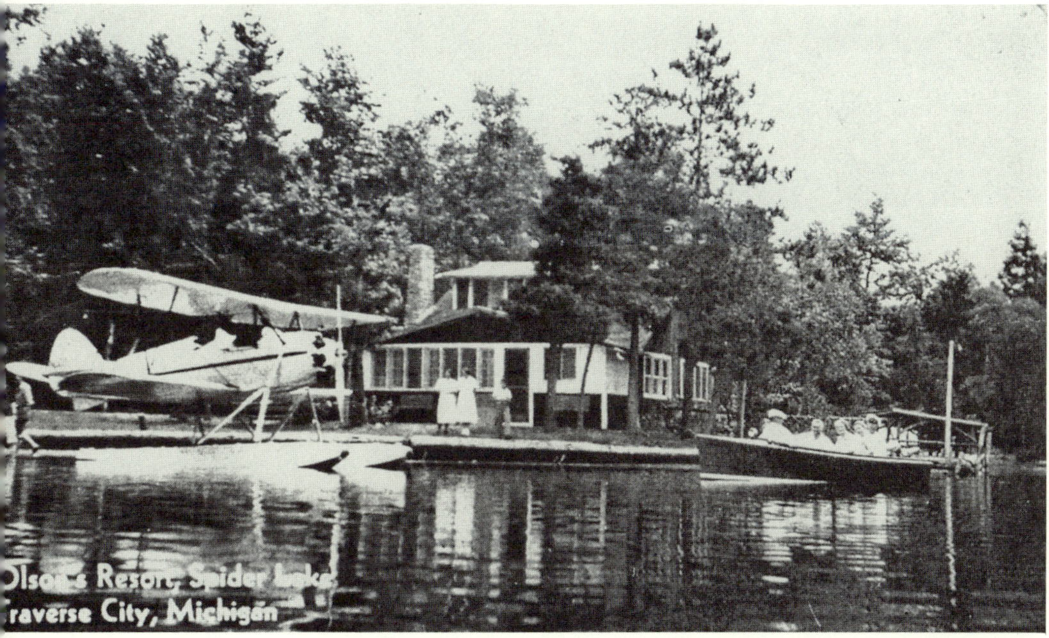

Olson's Resort, Spider Lake
Traverse City, Michigan

1938 photo.

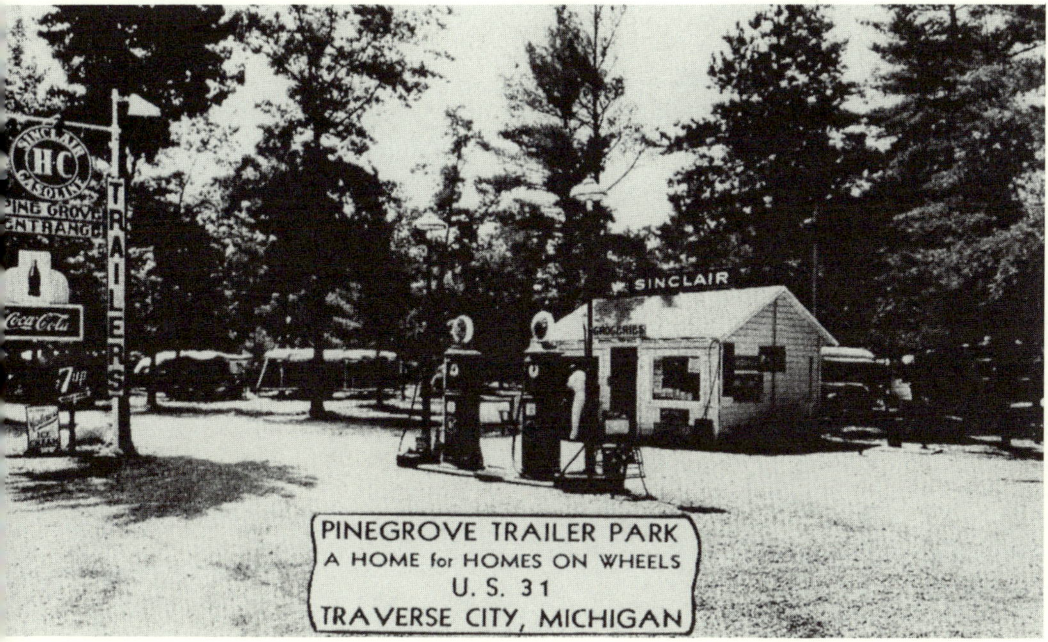

PINEGROVE TRAILER PARK
A HOME for HOMES ON WHEELS
U. S. 31
TRAVERSE CITY, MICHIGAN

PINE LANE CABINS ON U.S. 31 RT 14TH ST.
TRAVERSE CITY, MICH.
B-323

Shadowland Cabins
Summer of 1940
Traverse City Michigan

Boot Lake on Cass Street.

Popular dance pavilion on East Bay.

O-At-Ka Beach dance pavilion interior.

1926 Blossom Festival, Traverse City, Mich.

TRAVERSE CITY STATE Safety BANK Service

Straub & Amiotte float, 1926.

131.

Queen's Float, National Cherry Festival, Traverse City, Mich.

1934 Cherry Festival.

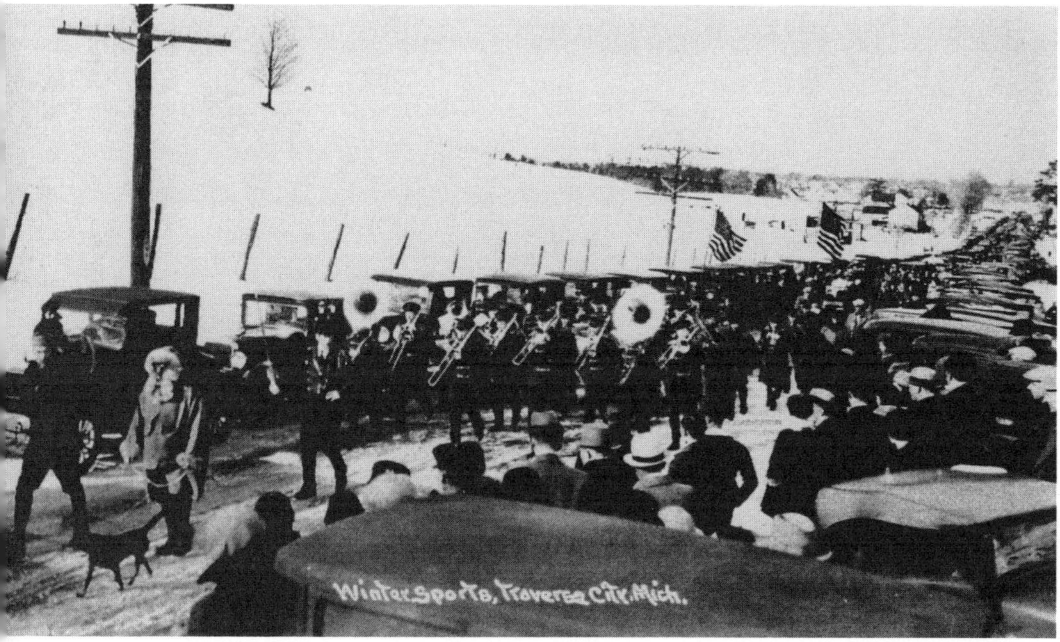
Winter Sports, Traverse City, Mich.

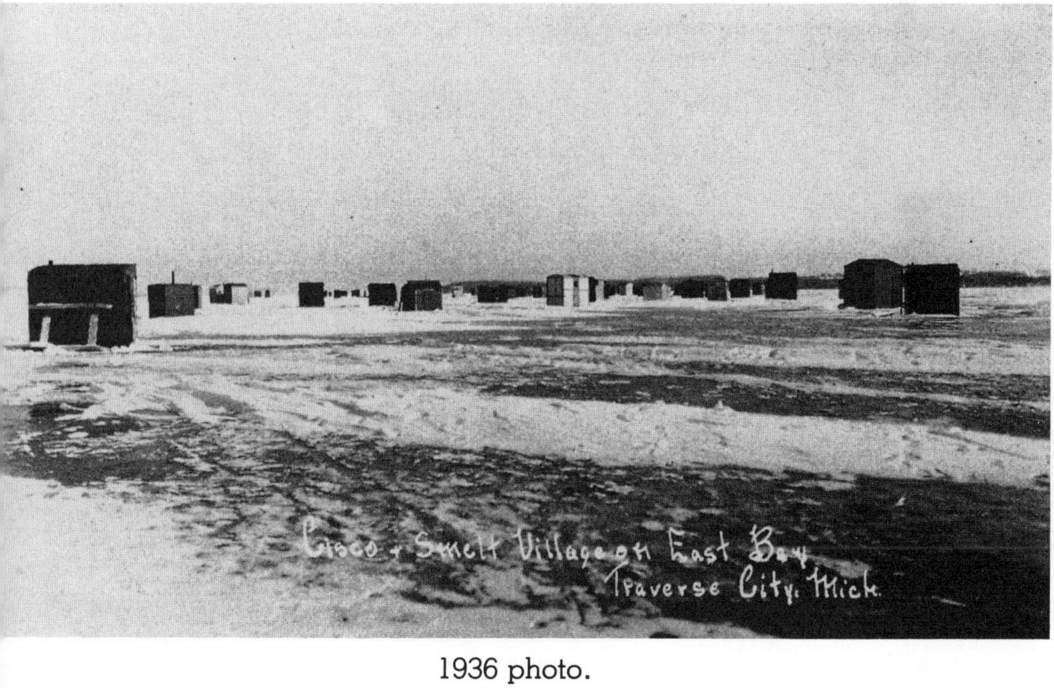
Cisco + Smelt Village on East Bay
Traverse City, Mich.

1936 photo.

Winter Carnival, 1936.

134.

135.

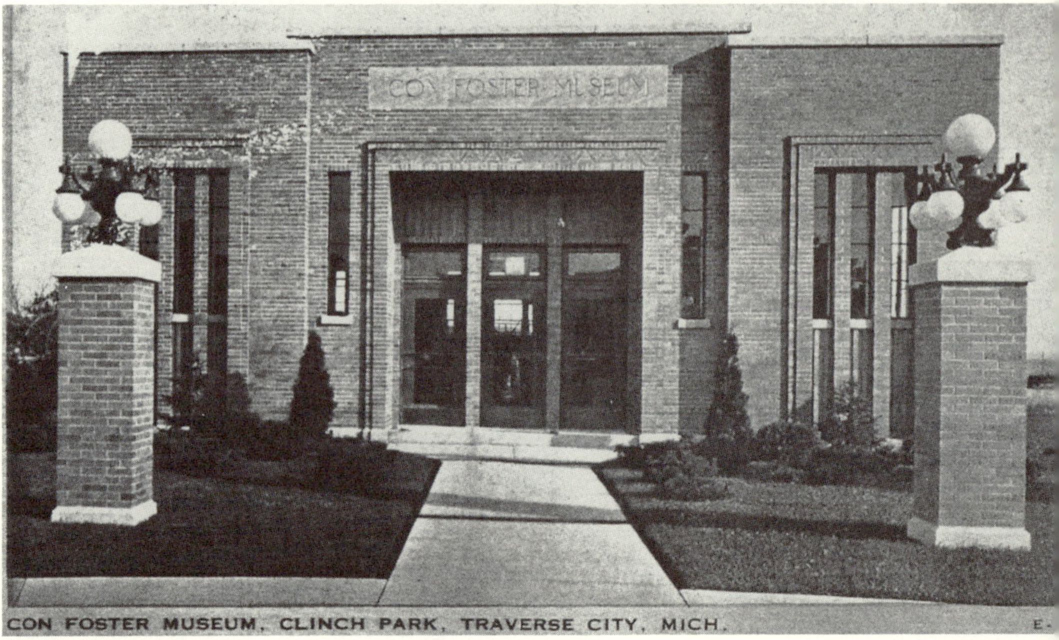

CON FOSTER MUSEUM, CLINCH PARK, TRAVERSE CITY, MICH.

Built in 1934.

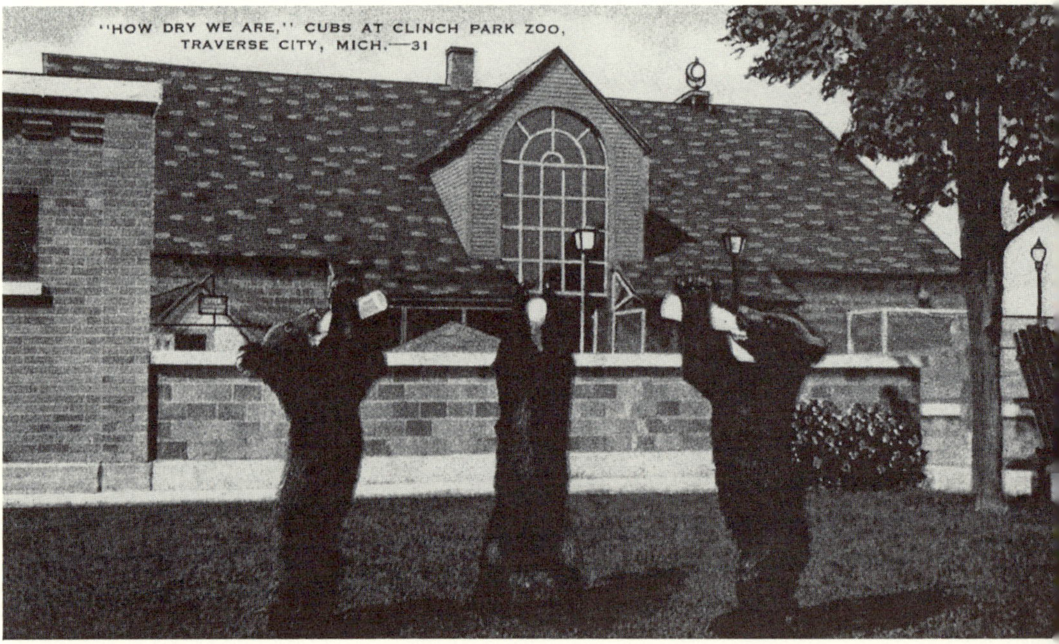

"HOW DRY WE ARE," CUBS AT CLINCH PARK ZOO, TRAVERSE CITY, MICH.—31

Big logging wheels at Clinch Park.

The Miniature City at Clinch Park, 1934.

AT THE ZOO, TRAVERSE CITY, MICH.—28

1934 photo.

Miniature City at Clinch Park, 1970s.

Shuffleboard clubhouse, East Front.

FRIEDRICH TOWER, GRAND VIEW ALONG PENINSULA DRIVE, TRAVERSE CITY, MICH.

EXTERIOR OF TRANSMITTER BUILDING SHOWING BASE OF 307 FT. TOWER, WTCM, TRAVERSE CITY, MICH.

1941 photo.

View from New Park Place Hotel, Traverse City, Mich.

1940 photo.

141.

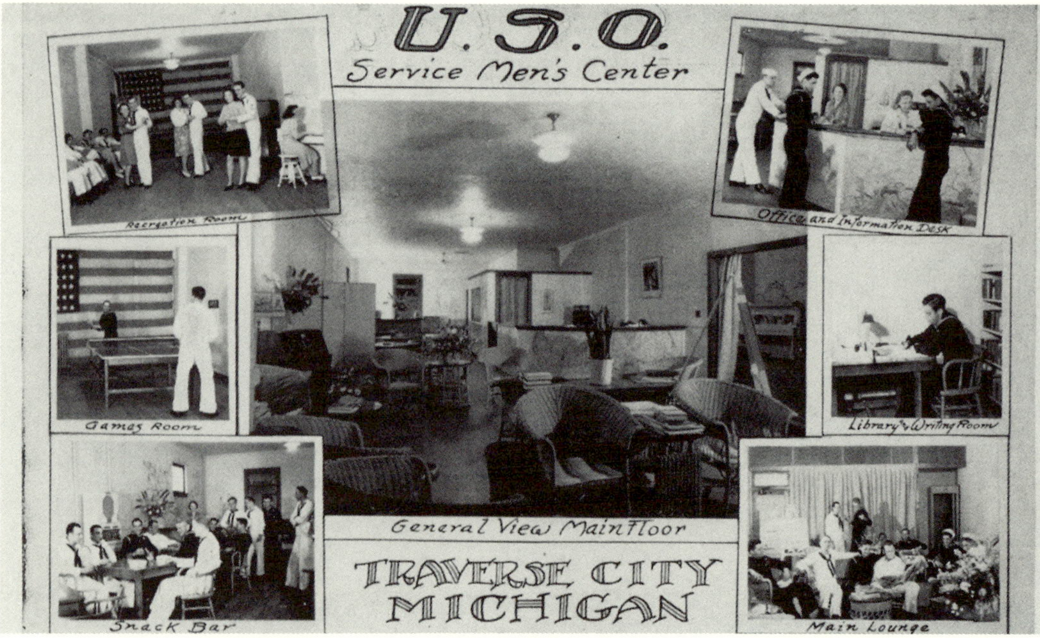

USO was in the Weaver Building at 118 South Union.

GT County Airport on Garfield Avenue, 1940s.

GRAND TRAVERSE COUNTY AIRPORT, TRAVERSE CITY, MICH. - 7

TC Shuffleboard Club courts.

1951-Present

Front Street 1950s.

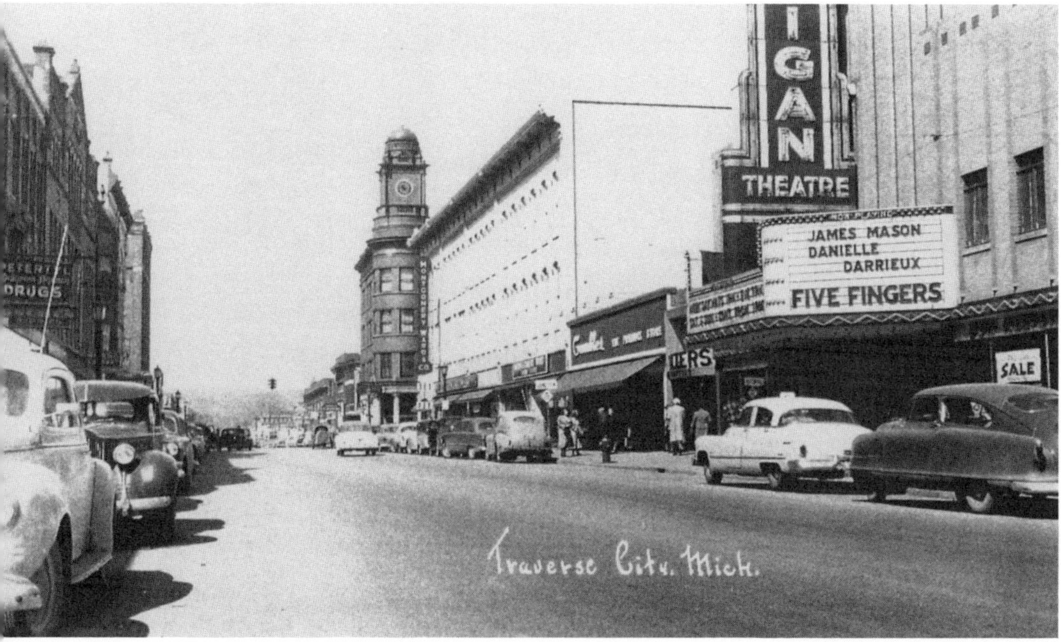
THEATRE
JAMES MASON
DANIELLE
DARRIEUX
FIVE FINGERS
DRUGS
SALE
Traverse City, Mich.

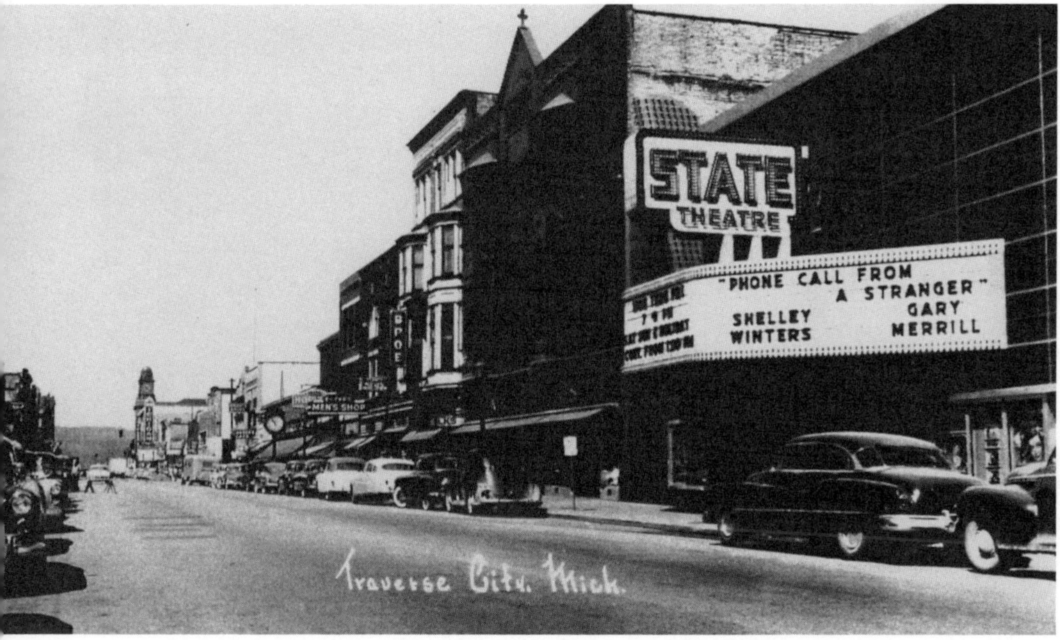
STATE
THEATRE
"PHONE CALL FROM
A STRANGER"
SHELLEY
WINTERS
GARY
MERRILL
MEN'S SHOP
Traverse City, Mich.

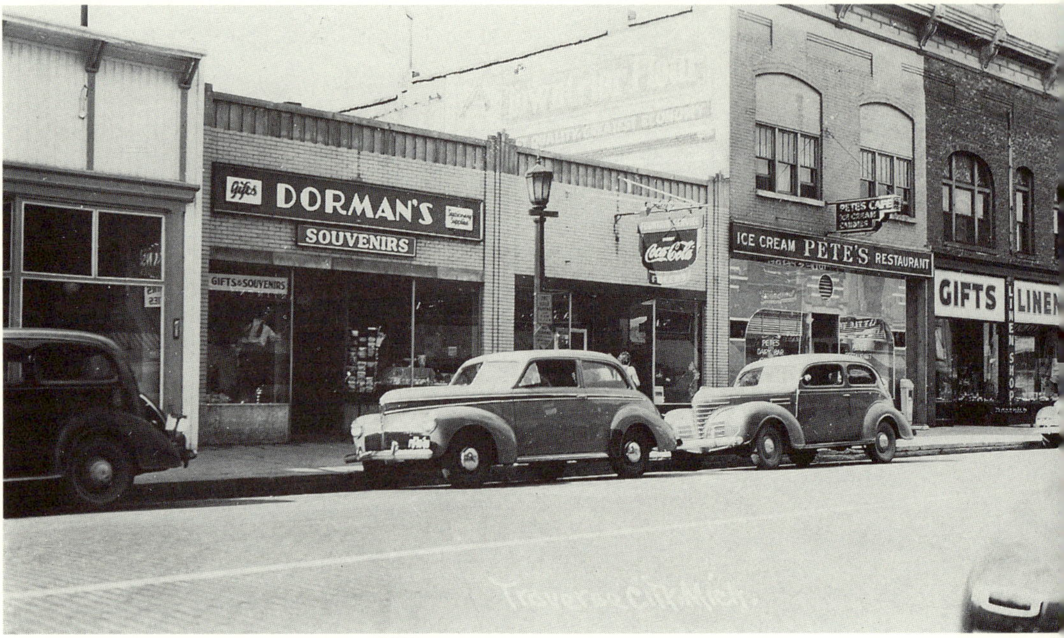
DORMAN'S
SOUVENIRS
GIFTS & SOUVENIRS
Coca-Cola
ICE CREAM PETE'S RESTAURANT
GIFTS
LINEN SHOP
Traverse City Mich.

Dorman's Gift Shop at 222 East Front.

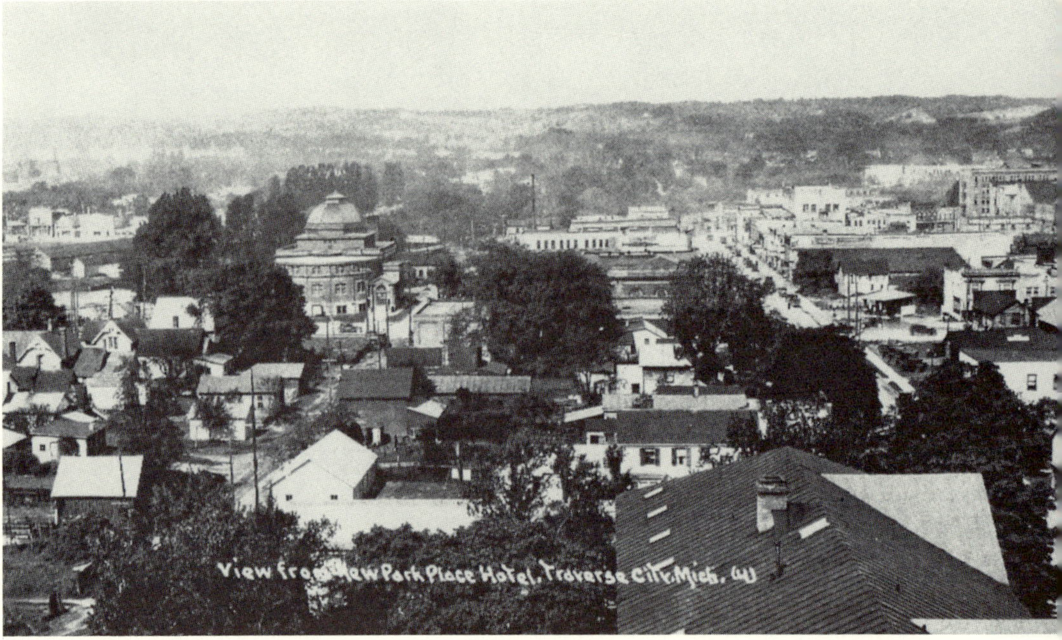
View from New Park Place Hotel, Traverse City, Mich.

Front Street, looking east.

Keystone Dam, 1951.

1970s photo.

Old Mission Lighthouse.

Park Place Hotel lobby.

Ed and Phyllis Bardy in their Latch String gift shop at 1215 East Front.

Shield's Restaurant on US-31 N.

The Osteopathic Hospital, Division and Bay, built 1949.

Union Street, looking north, 1960s.

Chamber of Commerce "block house", built 1965 on Grandview Parkway.

151.

Cherry Growers canning factory on West Bay.

Batsakis Inn on South Garfield.

DINING ROOM
BATSAKIS INN
TRAVERSE CITY, MICHIGAN

COCKTAIL LOUNGE
BATSAKIS INN
TRAVERSE CITY, MICHIGAN

Lampert's Drugs at 541 West Front.

Mark Osterlin Library was built in 1969.

Baker's Acres, 1960s.

Baker's Acres.

Cherry Festival parade, 1953.

Allegheny at Clinch Park marina.

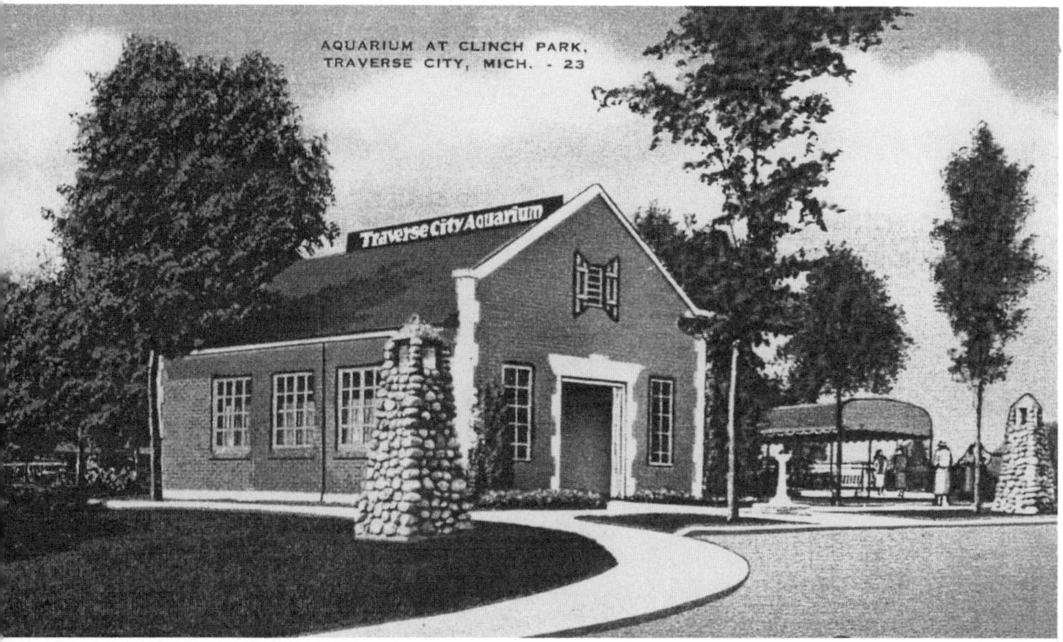
AQUARIUM AT CLINCH PARK,
TRAVERSE CITY, MICH. - 23
Traverse City Aquarium

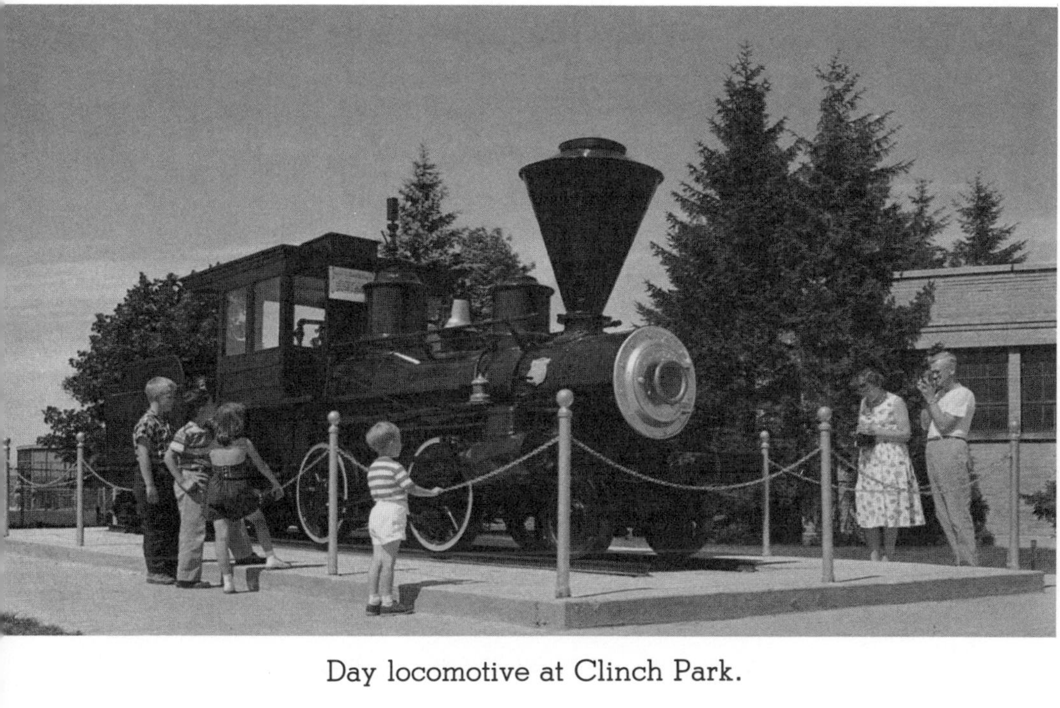

Day locomotive at Clinch Park.

Clinch Park.

Miniature railroad at Clinch Park.

Cherry County Playhouse opened 1955 in tent at State and Park.

Traverse City Golf & Country Club, 1960s.

Clinch Park marina, 1960s.